1 SUSSEX DRIVE

Gabrielle D'Emilio-Lappa

 FriesenPress

Suite 300 - 990 Fort St
Victoria, BC, V8V 3K2
Canada

www.friesenpress.com

ISBN
978-1-03-910445-7 (Hardcover)
978-1-03-910444-0 (Paperback)
978-1-03-910446-4 (eBook)

1. HISTORY, CANADA

Distributed to the trade by The Ingram Book Company

TABLE OF CONTENTS

This book is dedicated to John, my dear husband, in-house editor and best friend.

And to our sons, Roberto and Alessandro, for their love and support, especially during those Rideau Hall years.

"The universe is made of stories, not of atoms."

Muriel Rukeyser

ACKNOWLEDGMENTS

I started this "memoirs project" shortly after my retirement from Rideau Hall, where I had met and worked with so many inspiring and dedicated individuals. It was intended to be a simple collection, in a three-ring binder, of stories gathered during conversations over a cup of coffee or a casual lunch. Some recollections were still vivid, others had started to fade in the exactitude of their details, but they were all part of personal and memorable moments at Rideau Hall, shared with me by former colleagues and friends. I truly enjoyed hearing them and hope that my writing did them justice.

During the five years it took me to move from the "three-ring binder" format to a book, I was encouraged and inspired by some of these same people but also by others I had met throughout my career and in my personal life. To these people, I am truly grateful.

I would like to acknowledge and thank:

- Mrs. Gerda Hnatyshyn, for her inspiration and support and for showing me that important things are worth doing well;

- Richard Legrand, for his friendship and encouragement;

- the late Joyce Bryant, a mentor and friend who, before she passed, made me promise to finish writing this book;

- Michel Roy, former Rideau Hall photographer and friend, for his vision and assistance with the cover and the photos; Marie Glinski, Photography Coordinator at Rideau Hall, as well as

Bertrand Thibeault, Serge Gouin, Ronald Duchesne and the many other Rideau Hall photographers who, over the years, provided employees with invaluable memories through their photos, some of which are shared here;

- the Rideau Hall family and friends who shared their stories with me and provided hours of laughter and good memories;

- Gene Hattori, President, f-11 photographic design ltd., Saskatoon, for permission to use his photos taken for the book *"Rideau Hall, Canada's Living Heritage"* by Mrs. Gerda Hnatyshyn, C.C.;

- Sylvianne Latus, my former colleague, for her reviews, edits and good advice. Teaching an old dog new tricks was not easy;

- the Governors General and their spouses for whom I worked during my years at Rideau Hall and the Chancellery. It was an honour and a pleasure;

- and, finally, my former colleagues, who work at Rideau Hall and the Chancellery and who continue to care for the Office and the Residence and all that they represent.

To the memory of Claire Boudreau, historian, genealogist, Chief Herald of Canada, colleague and friend. Rest in peace. (1965-2020)

FOREWORD

Entering Rideau Hall in 1990, following my husband's installation as Canada's 24th Governor General, was both exciting and a little intimidating. While I had been a visitor to Rideau Hall in the past, seeing the staff assembled to greet us as the new occupants was an altogether different experience.

Rideau Hall staff have a myriad of responsibilities. They work tirelessly to ensure the lives and duties of the Governors General and their families are carried out with appropriate dignity. They offer every visitor, tourist and dignitary alike, a warm and respectful welcome. They ensure that the best of Canada is always on offer. Whether organizing tours, readying the majestic State rooms for ceremonies to honour Canadian achievement, caring for the finest Canadian furniture and art, selecting exquisite table settings or producing Canadian culinary delights, all are prepared, presented, and preserved to the highest standards.

While much has been written about the occupants of Rideau Hall, little has been written about the people (some with three, four and even five decades of service) who have been key to preserving the traditions and dignity of the Governor General's office. In the pages that follow, Gabrielle Lappa, a retired Rideau Hall staffer of some 36 years, has lovingly compiled and written a collection of memories and stories from her colleagues. Through their eyes, we are provided an intimate and animated glimpse behind the scenes.

Rideau Hall is a national treasure, thanks in no small measure to the dedication of these loyal men and women. While some 25 years have passed since I left Rideau Hall, I remain sincerely grateful to consider so many of the individuals who have shared their stories within these pages to be my friends.

Gerda Hnatyshyn, C.C.

The staff at Rideau Hall with the Rt. Hon. Ramon J. Hnatyshyn and Mrs. Gerda Hnatyshyn, 1995. Photo credit: Michel Roy

INTRODUCTION

"Together, you comprise a company of distinction and selflessness. Of early mornings and late nights. Of crises, national and international. Of tough choices and enormous tact. Of service to an institution that is as crucial as it is subtle and strong enough to change and to ensure stability for generations of your fellow Canadians. Throughout its history, this building has symbolized the best of what Canada has to offer – in its architecture and amenities, but even more importantly, in the quality of the men and women who work here." [1]

The Rt. Hon. Ramon J. Hnatyshyn

May 14, 1992

I t was Richard Legrand's first time back at Rideau Hall since he had retired as the maître d'hôtel, after more than 35 years of service with the Office of the Secretary to the Governor General. As we walked around and looked at the portraits of former occupants adorning the walls of the public rooms, he drew my attention to a portrait of

---

[1] Excerpt from a speech delivered by the Rt. Hon. Ramon J. Hnatyshyn on the occasion of the first employee reunion held at Rideau Hall, May,1992.

Norah Michener, the spouse of Governor General Roland Michener. He pointed to her slight smile. "See the corner of her mouth," he said, drawing my eye to a spot which appeared to be slightly blurred, unlike the rest of the painting. "When Mrs. Michener saw her portrait, she was not happy with it, because she was not smiling. So, she pulled out her lipstick, the same one she was wearing for the sitting and, with her finger, she dabbed a bit of colour onto the corner of the mouth, directly on the painting. She smeared it ever so lightly, so the lips suddenly seemed to have a subtle smile."

"That's better" she said. As I looked closely at the portrait, it was clear that there was, indeed, a slight smear on the painting, on the corner of Norah Michener's mouth. Who else could have known that? "I know because I was there when she did it" laughed Richard.

Rideau Hall, the official Residence of Canada's Governors General since confederation, has been host to some of the greatest leaders and dignitaries in history. Members of royal families, world leaders and heads of state have stayed here and have experienced, firsthand, the warmth and hospitality so often associated with Canadians. For those chosen to serve as Governors General, as well as for their families, Rideau Hall becomes their residence for five years, and sometimes longer. The Rt. Hon. Roméo LeBlanc called it "Canada's home," Adrienne Clarkson referred to it as "a living house," and David Johnston called it "the home of the people of Canada." But it is the ordinary Canadians who work with quiet dignity behind the scenes, and often for the greatest part of their working lives, who make Rideau Hall a home. These individuals are so invisible in their daily duties that they are hardly noticed, until they are missed. Many of them have been witness to historic events and memorable moments, some funny, some poignant and some surprising.

To the outsider, a visit to Rideau Hall as an invited guest is like watching a theatre performance, with the supporting cast and crew somewhere in the background but always where they are supposed to be. For those of us who worked behind the scenes, we felt that it could best be described as a window on Canada. The daily comings and goings could be quite ordinary or, at times, extraordinary. Regardless, in the words of former footman, then maître d'hôtel, Richard Legrand, "we were always 'live'."

During my own 36 years working with the Governor General's Office, I came to know and to watch these individuals, primarily as colleagues but also as friends – each bringing character, professionalism, loyalty, and intelligence to their work. The valet, the maître d'hôtel, the head housekeeper and others from this exclusive group were fiercely loyal to the institution they served but even more to the individuals who were temporary tenants in a Residence that has been home to more than 29 Governors General and their families. These staffers had one objective – to do their jobs well and to make Rideau Hall as welcoming and comfortable as possible for the residents and the guests. Their days often started at dawn and ended long after a regular workday. For them, working at Rideau Hall was a commitment and an honour. They were role models in their own roles.

This collection is not a historical presentation but rather a compilation of first-person narratives and real accounts of moments and periods in time, as lived and recounted by those behind the scenes, many of whom spent decades of their lives working at Rideau Hall. The stories were approved by the individuals being interviewed. My only regret is that size and time have prevented me from including the stories and memories of so many more of the dedicated staff members I've had the pleasure of working with and learning from throughout the years. There are many.

It is my hope that, through these stories, I am able to showcase, in some small way, the dedication and pride of those featured in the collection, to honour their unwavering loyalty and to preserve their legacies, which continue as part of the enduring traditions of life at Rideau Hall. I believe they need to be told.

Rideau Hall calligrapher, Barbara Lovelace, enhanced many invitations, notes and place cards with her artwork.

THE PEOPLE

"They see everything and hear everything but act as if they don't."

Alastair Bruce, Historical Advisor, Downton Abbey[2]

Quite often in our lives, we meet someone who, unknowingly, influences our choices and directions. Joyce Bryant, a dear friend, and one who is included in this collection, often referred to the "slender threads" that somehow connect us to one person, event or period which would then close a loop along our path. I never gave it much thought until I heard the story of how she ended up at Rideau Hall, working in different roles, for more than 40 years. In addition to Joyce, I was fortunate to meet a number of these individuals during my own thirty-six-year career at Rideau Hall. They guided and inspired me by their dedication and professionalism. I watched them and learned from them. The expectations I had for myself were set to match the standards of those who worked around me.

---

2   Alastair Bruce, Interview with Rosemary Jean-Louis, December 31, 2014

I learned to understand, by observation, the world of diplomacy and protocol. When I was 21 years of age, my first boss, Edmond Joly de Lotbinière, taught me the fine art of letter writing. We handled the invitations extended to the Governor General. Mr. de Lotbinière felt that every person or organization that had taken the time to write, deserved an acknowledgement and a reply, regardless of whether or not the invitation was going to be accepted or declined. In fact, he had such a way with words that he could write a letter declining an invitation which made the recipient feel almost as good as if the answer had been "yes." I learned early on, from those around me, that words and details mattered.

The people I have chosen to write about in this collection of life stories are just a few among the many outstanding colleagues I have worked with along the way. They provided guidance and support to each and every event, whether it took place at Rideau Hall, at the Citadelle in Québec or elsewhere in Canada or in the world. Their commitment to excellence for Canadians and their loyalty to the Office are notable. Time and space prevent me from including them all.

Joyce Bryant started her career at Rideau Hall as an assistant to Lord Alexander, the last British Governor General. She then went on to become a secretary for the first Canadian-born Governor General, the Rt. Hon. Vincent Massey. Joyce travelled with Mr. Massey and his family, worked at Buckingham Palace during their travels to the UK, was witness to discussions about state matters, royal visits and the creation of the Order of Canada, one of our country's highest civilian honours. She went on to become the first permanent employee of the Order of Canada Secretariat, bringing with her a wealth of first-hand knowledge and experience. Above all, her loyalty to the Office and her sense of humour made Joyce an invaluable and highly respected member of the staff at Rideau Hall.

Yves Chevrier, a humble and dedicated member of the Royal 22è Régiment in Québec, was chosen by General Georges Vanier to be his trusted valet or, as they referred to the position at the time, his "batman." Often described as the man behind the General, Yves took care of every detail of this war hero's public persona. From his uniforms and medals to always ensuring that his "spare wooden leg" was close by, just in case, Yves was also the only person who was with General Vanier when he took his last breath. He remained with Madame Vanier for a short time after and then continued his service to other Governors General.

Richard Legrand was 17 when he first walked up the long drive to the Residence for a job interview. Following a quick meeting with the Chief Steward and a "once over," which determined that the uniform would probably fit, he was told to show up the next day to start his new job as footman for the Micheners. He went on to become the maître d'hôtel for an additional 18 years, teaching and mentoring many about the fine art of service and hospitality.

The determination and strength of a young woman named Marion O'Brian is evident throughout her more than 40 years of service to 10 governors general. At the urging of her mother, Marion left her family and home in Jamaica to come to Canada looking for a better future. When she became aware of a job opportunity at Rideau Hall, she walked up to the front door, "because that is how it is done in Jamaica." Her experience working at the Jamaican Prime Minister's Residence, along with her self-confidence, landed her a position with the housekeeping team, also referred to as "the maids". In her more than 40 years of service, she has provided assistance to most members of the royal family and countless world leaders. It was a well-known fact that Marion was Queen Elizabeth's favourite when Her Majesty visited Ottawa, always leaving her with a token of appreciation for her service.

Marcel Smit started as a young orderly at Rideau Hall. His job description included sorting and delivering the mail throughout the Residence, printing daily arrangements and programs for events and "door man" to the VIPs and guests coming through the front doors of the Residence. He was responsible for raising the vice-regal standard flying atop the roof of Rideau Hall when the Governor General was in Residence and for lowering it when they were away. Before long, Marcel had learned so much about the workings of daily life at Rideau Hall that he became the "go to guy" for anything that needed attention, from facilities management to fixing a simple cable. Even the Governor General knew that Marcel would know where to find something or fix anything in the big house! Marcel was for all who knew him the epitome of service and dedication. "Not my job" was not in his vocabulary.

Along with these dedicated individuals are those who, through their stories of memorable moments from their years at Rideau Hall, provide a glimpse into the workings behind the scenes of Canada's top Residence. They each have their charm and take us back to simpler times.

It was 1992 when, at the invitation of the Right Honourable Ramon J. Hnatyshyn and Mrs. Gerda Hnatyshyn, the former and current staff members from Rideau Hall gathered for the first ever employee reunion. More than 500 former employees responded to the invitation and the event itself was history in the making. The employees were asked to pen one or two stories of their time at Rideau Hall. I am grateful to Mrs. Hnatyshyn who has agreed to share these and, although some of the authors are now deceased, I hope to honour them by including their stories here.

THE PEOPLE

Yves Chevrier, Trusted Valet – 51 years

Richard Legrand, Footman to Maître d'hôtel – 35 years

Joyce Bryant, Secretary and Confidante – 40 years

Marion O'Brien, Housemaid to Head Housekeeper – 46+ years

Marcel Smit, Orderly and Facilities Management – 36 years

Gilles Carrière, Footman to Maître d'Hôtel – 50 years

Tim Roberge, Pantry Helper to Head Footman – 41+ years

JoAnn MacKenzie, Director, Finance – 20+ years

Francine Bellanger, Plans and Protocol – 31 years

Louis Charest, Executive Chef – 21+ years

Lieutenant-General (retd.) Mike Hood, Aide-de-Camp

Chantal Charbonneau, Administrative Assistant – 31 years

Bernard St-Laurent, CD, from Aide-de-Camp to Deputy Secretary

Danielle Dougall, Assistant Director, Decorations and Medals –
29 years

Patricia (Tracey) McRae, Research Officer, Information Mgt. –
37 years

Kristina Jensen, Order of Canada Analyst – 20 years

Louise Cléroux, Secretarial assistant to the Secretary – 23 years

Garth Hampson, RCMP (ret'd) and volunteer at Rideau Hall –
51 years

…and others

LOYALTY AND DEDICATION

"...General Vanier had a remarkably devoted valet who had come from the Canadian Forces and he'd been with General Vanier throughout his regime. His name was Sergeant Chevrier. In the last days before his passing, Yves had been at General Vanier's side night and day, and when General Vanier died, he transferred his loyalty to Madame Vanier and looked after her in Montréal, before returning to Rideau Hall."

Esmond Butler, Secretary

Source: Esmond Butler, An interview with Tom Earle, Library of Parliament, September 9, 1988

YVES CHEVRIER, THE TRUSTED VALET

It was 1959 and, at the time, I was a member of the Royal 22ᵉ Régiment in Québec. General Vanier was the Honorary Colonel of the Regiment and, when he was appointed as Canada's 19th and first francophone Governor General, he asked for someone from the Regiment to come and work for him. I was one of a few candidates interviewed by General Vanier and I was honoured when he selected me to be his "batman", a military term for "valet." General Vanier, who had fought in the First World War, was 71 when he was appointed to the Office. Not surprisingly, this was not his first time living at Rideau Hall. General Vanier had served as an aide-de-camp to then-Governor General Lord Byng in 1921, almost 40 years earlier! Unlike me, he was very familiar with the demands and responsibilities which came with the title.

When I first arrived for my interview at Rideau Hall, the General asked me how old I was, to which I replied that I was 24 years old. His response was "You're just a child!" Little did I know that I would spend the greater part of my adult life working for this Office.

Those first few months were quite an adjustment for me. I did not speak English and I did not know anything about protocol. I had no specific training as a valet, although I had learned, early in my military career, to be very orderly and precise about anything that I was responsible for. Arriving at Rideau Hall, I felt like I was walking into a "château", but I was not nervous, because I knew the General and I also knew that he was a very kind, gentle man.

I learned early on that protocol was very important at Rideau Hall. I always addressed the Governor General and his spouse as "Excellences," the French term for "Excellencies," the correct salutation for these positions. The staff would often use a shortened version, referring to the Governor General as H.E. (His Excellency) when he wasn't around but, fearing that I might one day use this term when General Vanier was within earshot, I preferred to stick to the proper title.

A typical day at Rideau Hall started with my trip to the kitchen to pick up the General's breakfast and serve it to him in his room. As he was disabled, it was easier for him that way. He had lost a leg during WWI and, as a result, he had a wooden leg. When we travelled, I always carried a "spare leg" in a long wooden box, which was often mistaken for a weapon!

The days were filled with meetings, receptions and formal dinners. I would spend hours preparing the many changes of clothing that the General required, trying to anticipate all his needs. My job was to work behind the scenes, and I worked as needed, seven days a week. Most of my time was spent working directly for the Governor General and, occasionally, for Madame Vanier, although she had her own dresser.

The Vaniers worked well together. While General Vanier was calm, Madame Vanier, who was 10 years younger, loved to meet people and have animated discussions. She took charge of the Residence and enjoyed overseeing the decorating and refurbishing of some of the rooms. When General Vanier's health began to fail, she would often take his place at events such as school openings, visits and receptions. She was a great lady and had a wonderful personality. They were the perfect couple for this role. They truly complemented each other.

Yves Chevrier, trusted valet to eight Governors General and employee of Rideau Hall for more than 50 years. Photo credit: Gene Hattori, photographer

In addition to all their public events, the Vaniers would attend daily Mass in a chapel that had been set up in a spare bedroom in 1959. A large 18th century wooden chest, which they had purchased in France, served as the altar. They also owned a beautiful large crucifix which was placed in the chapel. Along with my role as valet, I was responsible for preparing the priest's vestments and assisting with serving the Mass. As devout Catholics, their faith was important to the Vaniers, and it grew increasingly more so as the years went on.

During the mandate, I accompanied the Vaniers on more than 100 tours across Canada. Most of their travels were aboard the vice-regal train. There were two designated railcars which included formal spaces to receive and entertain guests, a kitchen, sleeping quarters and office space. The team that travelled with the Vaniers worked well together and, like a family, we helped each other out. Our bedrooms had bunk beds that were stored away each morning to convert the space into offices during the day.

In the course of our daily duties, or even at night, it was not unusual to end up on the floor during a sharp turn or sudden stop! We were often on the road for weeks at a time.

General Vanier's health began to fail in the early 60s. On April 8th, 1963, election day, the General suffered a mild heart attack. That evening, he learned that the Liberals had defeated the Conservative government and he knew that the swearing-in of Lester B. Pearson would happen a few days later. With General Vanier's agreement, the ceremony took place in the Governor General's bedroom. As the Prime Minister-designate arrived shortly before noon, I recall His Excellency greeting him by saying "Good morning Mr. Pearson." Shortly after the noon ceremony had ended and Mr. Pearson had been sworn in, General Vanier said his farewells with "Good afternoon, Mr. Prime Minister." It was a touching moment for both men.

When General Vanier made a full recovery from his heart attack, Mr. Pearson asked him to remain in Office, at first for one additional year and then again until after the Centennial Year was over. Those next few years were challenging ones for the Vaniers, as signs of cultural discord and political unrest became more evident. The assassination of President Kennedy in the U.S., violent protests in the streets of Montréal and calls for the separation of Quebec from Canada were worrisome for a man whose spirituality and commitment to the unity and stability of his country had always been his primary focus.

During Centennial Year, more than 60 heads of state were expected to visit Canada. Although Madame Vanier took on an increasing number of events, General Vanier could no longer travel and was forced to reduce the level of activity in his program. One Saturday evening in early March, the Prime Minister visited the Governor General. They watched the hockey game together and spoke about the year ahead. It was clear that the Prime Minister was concerned about his friend's health.

During those final days, I was with General Vanier from morning until night. It was my job to be there for him and I know that it was comforting for the Vaniers to have me close by. On March 5th, 1967, the family had just left the bedroom to attend Mass in the chapel. Earlier that day, we had moved the General to a bedroom opposite the chapel and I had placed a large mirror on the door so that he could see the altar from his bed. When only the two of us remained in the room, General Vanier looked at me and said, "don't leave me alone." As I stood by his side, rearranging the oxygen mask he was wearing, he looked at me and said "Merci Chevrier." Shortly after, he closed his eyes and passed away. It was a moment I will never forget. He was a great man.

Following his passing, General Vanier lay in state in the Ballroom at Rideau Hall and then on Parliament Hill. The casket was draped with the Canadian flag and Madame Vanier asked that their crucifix, which had been in the chapel, be placed near the casket. As the funeral procession moved from Parliament to the Notre-Dame Cathedral on Sussex Drive, there was a seventy-eight-gun salute, one shot for each year of the General's life. It was a difficult day for all of us.

After General Vanier's funeral, Madame Vanier asked me to move to Montréal to help her get settled in her home. I remained there until 1974, when Jules Léger was appointed as Governor General, following Roland Michener's term. I was invited to come to Rideau Hall to meet Mr. Léger who explained to me that he was looking for a valet but that the job would not be very demanding since he was quite self-sufficient. Unfortunately, he suffered a debilitating stroke six months after his appointment. Mr. Léger had travelled to Sherbrooke, Quebec, with his brother, the late Cardinal Paul-Emile Léger, where he was to receive an honorary degree from the University of Sherbrooke. I did not accompany them since it was only a short trip but, as soon as I heard the news, I travelled to Sherbrooke to be with the Légers. Madame Léger's strength and determination during this time was extraordinary. She became her husband's shadow, speaking, reading and writing for him, and assisting him with the Speech from the Throne to open the new sessions of Parliament.

With successive mandates, our days seemed to become busier. Although I spent most of my time at Rideau Hall working as the valet, I did spend a few years in an office position during the Schreyer mandate. The Schreyers arrived in Ottawa from Winnipeg in 1979 with four children under the age of 13. They brought with them people familiar to the family who would assist with their daily requirements. When Jeanne and Maurice Sauvé arrived in 1984, I was asked to return to the position of valet, where I happily remained until I retired in 2010.

I recall 1992 being a particularly busy year, with the 125th anniversary of Canadian Confederation. The Rt. Hon. Ramon J. Hnatyshyn had taken Office two years earlier and 1992 included extensive travels across the country and participation in many special events. Mrs. Hnatyshyn took a great interest in Rideau Hall as a historical Residence, and she worked hard to elevate it to a standard comparable to other official Residences around the world. Along with the many projects and initiatives that she spear-headed, Mrs. Hnatyshyn provided opportunities for the staff to further develop their professional skills. So, when Richard Legrand (the Maître d'hôtel) and I were invited to Buckingham Palace to spend time with the kitchen, pantry and housekeeping staff, off we went! Once there, we were ensconced in the daily workings of Her Majesty's personal Residence where we were surprised to discover that things functioned very much like Rideau Hall, but on a larger scale! The experience was invaluable although we were told on a number of occasions that the staff at the Palace felt they had learned as much from us as we had learned from them.

One of the most important qualifications for the role of valet is discretion at all times. I did my best to protect the privacy of my employer and his or her family. They always knew that they could be themselves around me and that the trust would never be broken. Rideau Hall was their residence and their workplace for five years and sometimes more. It was our duty to make it their home.

Yves Chevrier with the Hnatyshyn pet bulldog, Sam. In addition to his role as valet, Yves often took over as the official guardian of the vice-regal pets at Rideau Hall. Photo credit: Bertrand Thibeault

As we approached the end of each mandate, it was always a difficult time for those of us who worked behind the scenes because of the trusting relationship that had developed over the years. Unfortunately, as one Governor General leaves, the new one arrives and there is very little time for emotions in between.

The staff at Rideau Hall was like a family for me. Everyone was dedicated to their work and we helped each other when needed. Our salaries were not high, but we also did not need very much. We were proud to work for the Governor General of Canada. That said, there were also some sad and difficult times, but there was always an underlying sense of loyalty, dedication and professionalism which carried us through.

I never thought I would remain with the Office of the Governor General for 51 years. When I turned 75, I felt that it was time to close the door on that stage of my life. I was fortunate enough to work for eight governors general and I always felt like I was a part of their families. I was with them during their busiest days, their challenging times but also during their most vulnerable moments. I admired them all and every one of them was an inspiration to me. It was an honour to serve them.

Yves Chevrier, C.M., R.V.M., CD

Yves Chevrier received the Order of Canada in 1980 and the Royal Victorian Medal from Her Majesty the Queen in 1994 for his years of service to the Crown. Photo credit: Michel Roy, photographer

"As I took dictation or just listened to Vincent Massey think out loud, I learned about history, literature, the social mores of different eras, and prominent personalities, alive and dead, – all accompanied by vivid mental pictures."[3]

Joyce Bryant

Joyce (Turpin) Bryant with the Rt. Hon. Vincent Massey.
(Personal collection)

---

3   Excerpt from *Slender Threads, A Memoir*, Joyce Bryant, Ottawa, 2007

JOYCE BRYANT, SECRETARY AND CONFIDANTE
(* with excerpts from 'Slender Threads, A Memoir' by Joyce Bryant, C.M., B.E.M.)

February 6, 1952 remains in my memory as a somewhat tumultuous day – our much-loved King George VI died, and Princess Elizabeth became our Queen. At Government House, our workload increased almost immediately, and extra staff was hired to help process the huge bags of sympathy letters that were arriving in the mail. Most social events were cancelled, and new, black-bordered official stationery was printed. All of this in the midst of a transition – Lord Alexander, the last British-born Governor General, was leaving on February 20th and Vincent Massey, the first Canadian to hold the post, was to be installed in an impressive ceremony in the Senate on February 28th. The break in tradition, from a British appointment to a Canadian, generated much controversy in the media, some of it quite vicious. Lord Alexander had been a revered wartime leader. Mr. Massey, by contrast, was a commoner, albeit a wealthy commoner, from one of Canada's elite families, with no overseas military service. Mr. Massey had lost his much-loved wife, Alice, the previous year, just 8 months before his appointment. It was a rotten way to start, with so many strikes against him, and the media were cruel in their coverage. To his credit, Mr. Massey worked extremely hard to overcome these obstacles.

Although my time at Rideau Hall began during Lord Alexander's mandate, I became Mr. Massey's personal secretary once he had settled into his new position, in addition to working for his son Lionel, who had taken on the role of Secretary to the Governor General. Because of the amount of work that needed to be done, this arrangement did not work very well. I must have lost seven pounds going up and down the stairs all day, between my office on the top floor and their offices on the main level! Although I was too nervous to reflect on it at the time, one of the most interesting eras of my life was about to begin.

I was born in Winnipeg in 1922. Although both my parents immigrated to Canada from England, at different times, they somehow ended up in the same boarding house and married a short time after they met. My childhood years were happy ones, until my father passed away when I was just fourteen. Financially, times were difficult for everyone due to the Depression and, before long, Mother and I were on a ship on our way to England. The days and months leading to the declaration of war in 1939 were a time of anxiety and frustration, waiting and preparation.

After the war started in earnest in mid-1940, I began to witness some of its horrific consequences. In 1943, the Royal Canadian Air Force (Women's Division) recruited in England for Canadian women and English wives of Canadian servicemen, so I enlisted and became the only Canadian on staff. I was posted to the Directorate of Medical Services in London, where I ended up working for the Director, Air Commodore Gordon Corbet who, several years later, would encourage me to take up my first position at Rideau Hall. But before then, the end of the war was drawing nearer and, once again, I witnessed first-hand this historic time. On VE Day, two things stand out in my mind – being part of the crowds in front of Buckingham Palace and seeing St. Paul's Cathedral lit up after so many dreary years of blackout. Nothing touched me so much or signified the end of those six terrible years so clearly.

As Canadian personnel began to be repatriated, I made a life-changing decision to return to Canada. I had lived through a lengthy war and seen much of the horror first-hand. I had wept at the loss of life and extensive destruction and I had worked every day for victory. I had survived air raids and lived through blackouts, strict rationing, and nights in air raid shelters. I had given thanks, many, many times for emerging from the conflict unscathed and not having lost any family members. I was now a competent, self-assured, well-trained young woman who had successfully served her country in the armed forces. It was now time to begin a new phase of my life.

I've always believed, throughout my life, that small, seemingly insignificant occurrences have led to enormous changes. Shortly after my arrival in Ottawa, I learned that I had been awarded the British Empire Medal (B.E.M) for 'outstanding efficiency displayed as an Orderly Room Clerk in the Directorate of Medical Services'. This came as quite a surprise as not many of these medals were awarded to Women's Divisions. The presentation took place at Government House (also referred to as Rideau Hall) on December 10, 1947, with His Excellency Lord Alexander presiding. This was my first introduction to Rideau Hall and, if anyone had told me that cold December afternoon that, a few years later, I would be working there, not only for Lord Alexander but also for seven other governors general, I would have unmercifully mocked them.

For the first few months in Ottawa, I worked at the Royal Canadian Air Force headquarters until the time for my discharge from the armed services approached. My mother, who had also returned from London, moved to Ottawa from Winnipeg and, for seven thousand dollars, we purchased our home at 102 Crichton Street, just a stone's throw away from Rideau Hall. Little did I know that I would spend the next fifty years of my life in this home and at Rideau Hall.

I continued my work for Air Commodore Corbet at RCAF Headquarters but there were not many prospects for promotion so, in early 1951, I wrote a public service exam that would make me eligible for promotion anywhere in the civil service. My results were not encouraging – I placed 29th out of the 30 candidates who took the exam! However, one day in October, someone at Government House called me for a job interview and, a few days later, I was offered a position which I accepted – another decision that would change my life dramatically!

I began my career at Rideau Hall in 1951, working as a clerical secretary to Lord Alexander of Tunis, a war hero who had been Governor General since 1946. Mr. Massey's appointment followed in 1952 and so began my career as his personal secretary.

Mr. Massey had a deep affection for Canada and its enormous potential, and he was tireless in expounding its virtues. He took great care in preparing his speeches, meticulous in his phrases and adamant about using a simple, short, expressive word rather than a long one. Normally, he dictated them to me, and I couldn't help but be grateful for those years spent at the Sir Isaac Pitman Institute mastering shorthand and other secretarial skills. As I took dictation from Mr. Massey, or just listened to him think out loud as he clarified his thoughts, I learned about history, literature, the social mores of different eras, and prominent personalities alive and dead – all accompanied by vivid mental pictures.

I was in my thirties during those early years at Rideau Hall – optimistic, full of beans, a little timid and given to giggling. When I was asked to join His Excellency for a vice-regal trip to the West Coast aboard the Governor General's train cars in September 1952, I was excited and yet apprehensive. I hadn't any idea what to expect or, more importantly, whether I could cope! I travelled with the crew on No.1

and 2 railway cars while His Excellency, Mr. and Mrs. Lionel Massey and their three young girls would fly to Regina to join the train and commence the tour. While on the train, the staff and crew were wonderfully kind to me. Wilfred Notley, the steward, Percy Corbin, the delightful round-bellied porter and the chef and pantry boys all looked after me as if I were family. We played lots of cribbage, until the official party arrived in Regina and the tour got into high gear. Along the way, His Excellency made numerous speeches at even the smallest whistle stops where crowds gathered to see the Governor General. I, on the other hand, spent most of my time in No.2 car, which also served as my bedroom. The workload rapidly increased and I quickly learned how to type on a moving, lurching train. At one point, we were rounding a bend at high speed and my steno chair, with me on it, shot out of the office into the corridor! The work never ended and even though there was little time to get off the train at major stops, I loved every minute of the six-week trip.

Travelling with the Governor General took me all over Canada and the pace was often hectic. It was not unusual to return from one trip, pick up fresh clothes and catch the train again for the next official visit. I was also fortunate to travel overseas with Mr. Massey who was a great friend of the Royal Family. In 1957, I accompanied the Governor General and his family on a trip to London which was to be part business and part holiday. Mr. Massey was holding discussions about the forthcoming visit of the Queen and the Duke of Edinburgh to Canada and the United States to open the St. Lawrence Seaway with President Eisenhower. We spent several weeks in London and I went between my hotel, Canada House and the St. James apartments where the Masseys were staying. I called it my "Piccadilly Beat!" During that time, I also worked for Colonel Charteris, the Private Secretary to Her Majesty, who was part of the discussions about the upcoming visit. It was at that time that I took the longest dictation of my career - twenty-nine pages of shorthand for a single letter! (I also got great pleasure from watching the actor playing Colonel Charteris on my favorite TV series, Downton Abbey!)

For the most part, my work wasn't glamorous, but the job did have its perks. Even though I was just one of many people that Mr. Massey saw and interacted with on a daily basis, I was a small cog in a big wheel which worked well. Every member of the team had an important role in supporting royal and state visits, as well as the many daily events in His Excellency's calendar. My work was rewarding, not only because of the Governor General but because of the marvelous, kind and competent colleagues with whom I worked who created a happy, collective feeling that permeated the environment. Everybody pitched in and there was little of "that's not my job." If something needed doing, you did it.

That said, the possibility of making serious gaffes was ever-present. During a visit to Chicoutimi, I typed the speech that His Excellency was to give that day and left it on his desk. A short time later, the vice-regal party left the train for the official welcome ceremony and, as I was tidying the Governor General's desk, I found the speech! Quickly commandeering an RCMP car, I rushed over to the site where the Mayor was introducing Mr. Massey as I tried to attract the attention of the aide-de-camp who kept frowning and shushing me. Finally, I waved the speech at him. Almost instantly, he paled, realizing that it was he who should have picked it up before leaving. He grabbed it and handed it to His Excellency, just as he was about to speak – a seamless event which could easily have turned out differently.

When Mr. Massey's term ended in 1959, I was sad to see the Masseys leave as they had been so kind to me. There were other opportunities for me at Rideau Hall such as doing budgetary estimates and administrative work, but I couldn't add two and two! Fortunately, shortly after Mr. Massey returned to Port Hope, his son Lionel called me and, in a roundabout way, asked me if I knew anyone who could fill the position of personal secretary for Mr. Massey. While it sounded like a wonderful opportunity for me, it would mean resigning from the civil service and moving to Port Hope – a big change at that time of my life. However, I was a secretary and that's what I loved doing so, less than two hours later, I began to prepare for another life changing move. I tendered my resignation at Government House and headed for Port Hope to join Mr. Massey again.

Back at home in Batterwood, Mr. Massey hosted a diversity of guests. Having been the High Commissioner in England during the war, he had numerous friends there, including members of the Royal Family, particularly the Queen Mother. When she came to stay at Batterwood, they would talk well into the night. The Duke of Edinburgh was also a visitor several times and, on one occasion, he asked me to type a speech for him. I did so and, when I returned it to him, he asked, "Did you find my handwriting difficult to read?" Without thinking, I blurted out, "Oh no sir, I've seen much worse!" I turned red with embarrassment, but Prince Philip roared with laughter.

By the spring of 1967, it was becoming apparent that there was less and less for me to do at Batterwood. Mr. Massey had just turned eighty and he had completed his major projects, including pressing for the establishment of a Canadian system of honours. The volume of daily correspondence was dropping off considerably. At that point, Hart Massey came to visit his father and took me aside, encouraging me to think about returning to the civil service. The federal government was not hiring anyone over forty-five and, as I was turning forty-five in a few months, I should act soon, or it would be too late.

In the meantime, the sudden passing of General Vanier, Mr. Massey's successor, led to a quick transition when the Rt. Hon.

Roland Michener was recalled from his posting as the Canadian High Commissioner in India to become our 20th Governor General. With this in mind, I went to Ottawa to celebrate Dominion Day (Canada Day). It was our centennial year, and I had an appointment with then Secretary to the Governor General, Esmond Butler, at Government House. I wanted to speak to him about the possibility of coming back to Rideau Hall. Specifically, I had hoped that there might be a place for me working with the group that was developing the protocol and procedures for the new honours system and the Order of Canada. In April, Prime Minister Lester Pearson had announced in Parliament that the Order of Canada would be "born" on July 1, 1967. There would be much to do to get it up and running and the thought of helping to lay the groundwork excited me. Mr. Massey had long advocated for a distinctly Canadian honours system, and I had been party to his many discussions with the Prime Minister's Office and Mr. Butler at Government House. So, I felt that I could bring a lot of background to this new endeavor.

A few days later, Mr. Butler called to tell me that I had been hired to work in the new Order of Canada Secretariat. The job description was understandably vague, as it had never existed before, and everyone involved was desperate to get going. I was elated – and I had a job back in a place that I knew and loved! And so, I began my 2nd chapter at Rideau Hall in August 1967.

The Prime Minister's April announcement introducing the Order of Canada had created quite a buzz. Popular sentiment supported an honours system that was uniquely Canadian and honoured citizens from all walks of life, not just the military. A staff of five was seconded from different government departments to work at Government House and to bring the Order of Canada into being. I joined this group as the first permanent member of the Secretariat.

A year earlier, Prime Minister Pearson had personally and secretly assigned Bruce Beatty, a highly skilled graphic artist at the Department of National Defence, to design an insignia for the Order. Bruce's final design was a six-armed snowflake with a maple leaf in the centre. He chose a snowflake as the symbol for the Order, since each snowflake is as unique as each member of the Order. In later years, the design took on a deeper and more important meaning to me. I saw it as the outward symbol of the collective contributions made towards a "better country" by more than five thousand Canadians from all walks of life and representing every region of the country. Their diverse accomplishments, represented by the six arms of the snowflake, come together to create a common good – a better country.

Those last few months of 1967 were exciting and exhilarating as we were under a great deal of pressure to finalize all the work before the first investiture, which was to be held on November 24th. There were few precedents to draw on – certainly none in Canada. It was decided that the ceremony would generally follow the format used at Buckingham Palace; but apart from that, every decision was another step into the unknown. An Advisory Council was convened, chaired by the Chief Justice, and having as its members the heads of the Privy Council and the Under-Secretary of State, as well as representatives from various prominent organizations. The Council began to review the many nominations that were received, and 90 Canadians were on the final list for that first investiture. Our life became truly frantic as we tried to organize everything – from accommodations to travel arrangements and the countless details for the investiture itself. While the job was hectic and stressful at times, it was immensely satisfying, especially when we got it right. And frustrating when we didn't. At the end of an investiture, we were exhausted!

My former boss and dear friend, the Right Honourable Vincent Massey, was among that first group of Companions appointed to the

Order, and it must have given him the greatest pleasure to see the recommendations that he had made over the years coming to fruition. During his stay at Government House as a guest of the Micheners, he invited me to have a sherry and a chat. It was grand to see him again and he surprised me with gifts of a lovely 17th century inscribed silver tea caddy, as well as a pair of Sheffield candlesticks. We had a wonderful visit, with no indication that this would be the last time I would ever see him. Shortly after the investiture, Mr. Massey flew to London for Christmas. Tragically, he fell ill, and, despite the best of care, he died on December 30th. What sadness. He had meant so much to me.

While I loved my job, any mistake or seemingly harmless oversight could have disastrous consequences. No matter how well we planned and checked things and prepared for the unexpected, something unforeseen would often threaten the process! For my part, I was directly responsible for a few snafus! In the early 1970s, the Order of Canada had only two levels: Companion and Medal of Service. One day, I inadvertently mixed up two letters. The first went to Dr. Gerhard Herzberg offering him the lesser Medal of Service – obviously a mistake as Dr. Herzberg was one of Canada's outstanding scientists and had just won the Nobel Prize for Chemistry. The second letter, offering the honour of Companion, was sent to a woman who should have been offered the Medal of Service. When I realized what I had done, I nearly fainted! After recovering, I ran upstairs and burst into Mr. Butler's office, blurting out "I've done the most awful thing and there's nothing you can say to me that I haven't said to myself!" I explained the situation. Mr. Butler was aghast but listened to my proposed solution which was to call both the recipients to explain the mix-up. I explained to them that the error was entirely mine and that neither the Governor General nor the Advisory Council had anything to do with it. Both individuals were most understanding and accepted my explanation and apology. In fact, when I talked to the woman who had been inadvertently promoted and then quickly demoted, she was more gracious and forgiving toward me than I deserved!

The investiture ceremonies also had their lighter moments. Typically, an investiture started with the ceremony in the Ballroom, followed by a reception and ending with a banquet. It was the custom of the Governor General to sit at one table and Her Excellency at another. Dinner was buffet style and the guests proceeded down both sides of long tables laden with hot and cold dishes. Subsequently, the dessert was set out with a variety of delectable choices. On one occasion, I was wearing a green and gold evening dress as well as some earrings, that I had borrowed from a friend. As I was moving along the dessert table among the guests who were filling their plates, I leaned over and, as I did, one of my earrings fell off and disappeared with a plop into the middle of a massive, beautiful, untouched maple mousse. Appalled, and with nightmarish visions of a guest behind me swallowing the earring while partaking of the mousse, I grabbed a large serving spoon and unceremoniously scooped up the entire centre of the mousse, slapped it on my plate and walked away as if nothing had happened – hoping that the chef, who was hovering nearby, had not seen me destroy his elegant creation! After returning to my table, the aide-de-camp, who was sitting next to me, gallantly retrieved the earring from the mousse and dunked it into his glass of water so that I could wear it again.

During another investiture, I was wearing an evening dress with a particularly long sash which tied at the front. At one point, while I was holding a Companion's badge which, at the time, cost hundreds of dollars, I accidentally stood on the end of the sash, which jerked my hand and sent the badge into the air. Fortunately, I caught it on its way down, as it would surely have cracked had it hit the floor. And, I would have had to explain to the recipient, whose appointment number was engraved on the back, why he wasn't getting his insignia that day!

As the 1970s drew to a close, I gave more thought to retiring. I had married late in life to my dear friend Bert Bryant and I looked forward to spending more time with my new husband. I decided to retire on July 4th, 1981 after thirty years of service to Rideau Hall. However, my freedom days were short lived as, soon after my retirement, I was asked to return to Rideau Hall to take on a few projects. I agreed to return to work for the Office and ended up staying for another ten years when, after serving eight governors general and celebrating Canada's 125th anniversary and the 25th anniversary of the Order of Canada, I felt that I had been witness to enough milestones and memories to take me into my final retirement in 1992. I ended my career at Rideau Hall with the delightful task of helping to organize a reunion for current and former employees of Government House which was attended by hundreds of colleagues and friends. It was like a family reunion, seeing those individuals with whom I had spent long days, countless hours, holidays and birthdays, and who were, for me, my Rideau Hall family. I knew then, as I know now, that I was truly blessed to have had them in my life.

Looking back, I can honestly say that I've had a good life and a wonderful career. And for more than half of those years, I was privileged to work for the Queen's representative in Canada. I say privileged because I have worked with and for many distinguished Canadians, witnessing moments of history and the evolution of some of our country's key institutions. For this, and for those who mentored me and cared for me along the way, I am truly grateful.

Joyce Bryant

Joyce Bryant was awarded the British Empire Medal (Military Division) in recognition of her meritorious service throughout the war. She was also appointed to the Order of Canada in 1973 for her long service to the Office. Joyce passed away in November 2017, at the age of 95. Photo credit: Ottawa Citizen

Excerpts from *Slender Threads, A Memoir*, Joyce Bryant, Ottawa, 2007

"Joyce Bryant, Mr. Massey's private secretary, always provided a ready and friendly answer to our questions. On more than one occasion, she saved us much embarrassment by quietly pointing out that it would be better not to invite Mrs. "X" and Mr. "Y" to the same dinner party, let alone to sit them next to each other, as they had previously been married to each other.... but now had different spouses."[4]

Hamish D.W. Bridgman, Aide-de-Camp, Massey regime

---

4   Source: Hamish D.W. Bridgman, ADC, Massey Regime, Excerpt from Employee Reunion collection, 1992

AN UNEXPECTED SUMMONS

It had been a difficult day at work – work being the Secretariat of the Order of Canada at Rideau Hall. So many letters to send out and each one had to be perfect. I was tired, my back and knees hurt, and I wanted to go home. Darkness had already fallen, and the bleak autumn weather looked singularly uninviting.

"Miss Turpin, I need to see you in my office right away!" Was that really the Governor General barking at me over the intercom? What could possibly have upset him? His Excellency was usually such an easy going individual – unfailingly polite and courteous. And why did he want to see me? My duties with the Order rarely brought me in contact with him. What had I done?

Panic and anxiety taking hold, I rushed up the stairs as fast as my poor knees would permit, searching my heart and mind for whatever could have earned Mr. Michener's displeasure. While I loved my job, any mistake or seemingly harmless oversight could have disastrous consequences. A few years earlier, I had inadvertently mixed up some letters from the Secretariat, offering an appointment as a Companion of the Order to an individual, when that letter should have gone to Dr. Gerhard Herzberg, a Nobel Prize winner. A gut feeling told me that, this time, the offence, whatever it was, was much more serious.

My timid knock on the door of Mr. Michener's study was greeted with a terse "Come in!" Entering, I was confronted with a grim-looking Governor General and, to my horror, my immediate supervisor, Roger Nantel, and the Secretary General of the Order, Esmond Butler - both of whom were glaring at me in an unpleasant manner. No greeting or invitation to sit down. "So, this is it," I reasoned. "Whatever I've done, it's beyond the pale and, rather than give me another chance, they're going to fire me!"

Then, I noticed a letter in His Excellency's hand - a letter that he seemed poised to read. The truth suddenly dawned on me. "How silly. They're not going to fire me – that would be much too messy. They've drafted a letter of resignation for me to sign. Much more practical. No public embarrassment for anyone; just a short announcement, the appropriate goodbyes and dutiful gestures of appreciation for a job well done, and I'll be gone."

Despair flooded my soul as a visibly upset Mr. Michener said, "Miss Turpin, I have a letter to read to you." Before I could say anything, he began reading. "Dear Miss Turpin, I am pleased to inform you that the Advisory Council of the Order of Canada has recommended to the Governor General that you be appointed a Member of the Order of Canada." And then he stopped; his demeanor changing completely and his face breaking into a broad warm smile – the delightful smile that I was so familiar with. What was going on? This wasn't a letter of resignation; it was the standard letter that the Secretariat sent out to individuals who had been nominated to the Order of Canada, asking them if they would accept. I knew that letter. I had typed hundreds of them. But this one was addressed to me! "I don't think I need to read you the rest of the letter, Miss Turpin. I'm sure you know it by heart." And then His Excellency rose and gave me a kiss, followed by Roger Nantel and Mr. Butler, who had similarly been transformed back into the kind, considerate souls that I knew them to be.

In a state of shock, I completely lost control of my emotions and burst into tears. Stepping back, I fell over the arm of a chair and landed on the floor in a spectacular fashion with my legs in the air! After I had recovered and was comfortably seated, His Excellency offered his congratulations and questioned me as to whether I had any idea that I was to be appointed to the Order. He had gone to great lengths to keep it a secret and was delighted to know that the efforts were a success.

On April 3, 1974, the Rt. Hon. Jules Léger invested me as a Member of the Order of Canada. My citation read "For her dedication throughout her service at Government House during the tenure of five governors general." As I sat among the other recipients, Canadians who had contributed to the betterment of our country in so many ways, I felt overwhelmed by emotions of joy and gratitude to be counted among them.[5]

Joyce Bryant receiving the Order of Canada from the Rt. Hon. Jules Léger in 1974. (Photo from Joyce Bryant's personal collection)

5   Excerpt from Slender Threads A Memoir, Joyce Bryant, Ottawa, pages 1-3

Large Dining Room at Rideau Hall (l to r) Footmen Charles Proulx, Jimmy (Gilles) Carrière and Claude Lepage with Maître d'hôtel Richard Legrand
Photo credit: Gene Hattori

BEGINNINGS

"When setting tables for official dinners, we used a measuring stick to ensure that the distance between each place setting was precisely the same. The same stick was then used to measure the distance from the edge of the table to each chair. Standing at the end of the stately dining room table, the place settings were perfectly lined up like the columns of St. Peter's Basilica in Rome."

Richard Legrand, R.V.M., Maître d'hôtel

RICHARD LEGRAND, FROM
FOOTMAN TO MAÎTRE D'HÔTEL

My interview for the job consisted of one question from the Chief Steward. "How tall are you?" I stood a little straighter and replied, "6 feet, 2 inches." "Good. I think the suit will fit you. You're hired." And that was how I started my career at Rideau Hall.

I was 17 years old when a family friend, who worked as a footman at the Governor General's Residence, suggested I apply for a position that was vacant. A footman is responsible for attending to the Governor General and the family's everyday needs, a world which was as foreign to me as anything "royal". I don't know if it was curiosity or innocence that encouraged me to apply for the position but, shortly thereafter, our friend, Marcel Breton, set up an interview for me. Off I went, not realizing that, once I stepped into that big grey mansion, it would become my home for the next 35 years.

I was born and raised in Hull, Quebec. My father worked at the EB Eddy paper plant and my mother worked at the Duvernay Hotel in Hull as a housekeeper. I left school when I was 16 and had little formal training other than working for a year at Jimmy's Tavern and Restaurant on Bank Street in Ottawa. My parents had recently separated, and my sister had left home to marry, so my mother and I were on our own. It was a difficult time and, with no schooling or stability, any job prospect was welcome. As a child, I would sometimes go with my mother to the hotel where she worked, helping her to carry the linens and watching as she made the beds and cleaned the rooms for the guests. She was meticulous in her work and

I truly believe that her standards instilled in me, at a young age, the need to see things done right.

I recall that when the call came for the interview, my mother was so happy, primarily because of the opportunity it might present for her son but also because of the possible break from a predictable and unstable future. It was November 1968 and Marcel told me that I should show up at Rideau Hall on November 11th, Remembrance Day. Although I had seen the outside of the Residence once before, the grey stone mansion beyond the gates was as far removed from my world as Buckingham Palace itself.

I didn't have a car so off I went, walking from Wellington Street in Hull, across the newly constructed MacDonald Cartier bridge. It was a grey, dreary November day and the Ottawa River, which had always been a backdrop to my childhood, today seemed to be the divider between my youth and adulthood. I continued down to Sussex Drive, walked by 24 Sussex, then Prime Minister Lester B. Pearson's residence, and crossed the street to the tall black iron fence that surrounded Rideau Hall. Surprisingly, nobody stopped me as I walked through the gates, past the RCMP officer. The Residence itself is not visible from the front gates so I began the walk up the seemingly endless winding drive until it appeared. It looked like someone had dropped this grey stone mansion in the middle of a park, far from the noise of the city. I stopped for a second to look at it but all I could think about was arriving at the right door, and on time. I was nervous.

I had been instructed to go to the "Trade Entrance" on the side of the building. The punch clock for the staff was next to the door and, ahead, was a staircase that led up to the pantry. Jean Villeneuve, the Chief Steward, was waiting for me at the top of those stairs. That was when he asked about my height and proceeded to hire me! Turns out that the suit pants were a bit short, but I got the job anyway! And November 11th was my first day.

Remembrance Day is a busy one for the Governor General. As the Queen's representative in Canada and the Commander-in-Chief, all events are focused on remembering the men and women who fought for and served our country. Once dressed, I was told to go and stand by the front door of the Residence. Of course, I had no idea where the front door was! I eventually found it and, as I was standing in place, I recognized the distinguished gentleman walking towards me, accompanied by an aide-de-camp. The Rt. Hon. Roland Michener, a former politician, Speaker of the House and diplomat had been called back from his posting as the Canadian High Commissioner in India to become our 20th Governor General, following the sudden passing of General Georges Vanier on March 5th, 1967. Standing tall but trembling inside, I held the front door open. As Mr. Michener was about to walk by me, I noticed that his medals were not hanging properly. They were crooked. I hesitated but then reached over to straighten them. Mr. Michener looked me in the eye and said, "And who are you?" I introduced myself and thus began a long and pleasant relationship with the Micheners.

As I walked home that first day, the span of the bridge back to Hull seemed a lot shorter and the air warmer even though the sun had already set. I didn't know what the future held for me but, after that day, I knew what I wanted for myself.

Rideau Hall is one of two official Residences for the Governor General of Canada, the second one being at the Citadelle in Québec. Also referred to as Government House, Rideau Hall was originally built in 1838 by renowned stonemason Thomas MacKay, who built a number of famous landmarks in Ottawa, including the locks of the Rideau Canal. This historic building has been home to every Governor

General since confederation. Throughout the years, the Residence underwent many transformations and extensions, most of them welcomed, but often presenting challenges for the residents as well as the staff! There are approximately 140 rooms at Rideau Hall including the Governor General's office, the spouse's office, private quarters for the vice-regal couple, living quarters for the military aides-de-camp, state rooms for official events, kitchens, an administrative wing, as well as a greenhouse. On the grounds, there are several other buildings including Rideau Cottage where the Secretary lives, a historic stable building which had previously been used for horses and carriages, a gatehouse near the entrance to the grounds, a garage for limousines and private apartments for some of the staff not living in the Residence. The accommodations on the grounds ensured that a chef or chauffeur, a valet or a housemaid could be summoned at any time.

On my second day, I was given a key to my room which was located on the lower level (the basement) of the Residence. My room included a single bed and a chest of drawers with a beautiful big window overlooking the private gardens at ground level. Even in the middle of our cold grey winters, the view was like a postcard. All six footmen lived there while the housemaids and cooks had their rooms on the top level, close to the private quarters, the pantry and the kitchen. We paid room and board – 50 cents a day – which was deducted from our pay cheques. This included meals, laundry, stamps, a train pass and a bottle of spirits once a month!

At the time, most of the staff at Rideau Hall was single. There were approximately 40 staff members working in the Residence and on the grounds, as well as 25 or so administrative staff. We spent so much time together that we were like an extended family, with the same expected amount of drama as a family but which was never visible to those we served.

It was understood that staff members would become a part of the daily functioning of the Residence and the concept of "nine to five" did not exist. The days consisted of early mornings and many long evenings. Sometimes we worked seven days a week, without a day off for months. During split shifts, we worked early mornings and stopped for a few hours after lunch was served. We would start again around 3 p.m. and continued until after dinner or until the Micheners retired. The schedule varied from one day to another and last-minute changes were par for the course. We learned early on that flexibility and adaptability were essential for the job!

I will never forget the evening when the Micheners were out for an event and returned quite late. As always, there was a footman at the door awaiting their arrival. It was my turn to take up the post by the door so off I went to the front of the Residence. However, standing by the door, I could barely keep my eyes open. I decided to sit on the staircase in the front foyer while awaiting Their Excellencies' return. Unfortunately, I dozed off and it wasn't long after that I heard loud knocking at the front door with the Micheners and the aide-de-camp peering inside the window, waiting to be let in. Needless to say, I did not sleep very well that night, fearing for my job, but I was told that Mr. Michener had a good chuckle about the incident!

As footmen, our job started at the crack of dawn, with one of us or the valet awakening the vice-regal couple. We would enter the room quietly, open the drapes and gently announce the time, which was usually about 6:00 a.m. Since Mr. Michener was a sportsman, he loved to jog early in the morning. He would come down the elevator, wearing his beret. A footman was always by the door when he left and when he returned to Rideau Hall. One morning, someone had parked their car by the door and had left the motor running. Mr. Michener did not like to see an engine idling for no reason—he was an environmentalist even back then! He stepped into the car, turned off the motor and left with the keys, leaving the poor individual no choice but to fess up so he could get his keys back from the Governor General himself.

Breakfast for the Micheners was always served in their private quarters. There were two ladies who worked in a smaller kitchen, adjacent to the main kitchen, who were responsible for preparing the breakfast trays. They were nicknamed "the steel ladies" because they were always in this small stainless-steel kitchen! Their jobs included rolling the butter curls or molding the small pats of butter into maple leaves, preparing coffee and tea trays as well as the small sandwiches for afternoon tea. Once the breakfast trays were ready, the footmen would bring them to the cooks who put the hot food on the plates, and we delivered them to the private quarters. The valet was usually there to bring in the trays. It was a well-oiled machine!

In addition to their daily schedule of events, the Micheners loved to have tea around 5:00 p.m. During the winter, tea was usually taken in the greenhouse, surrounded by beautiful blooming flowers and plants. They were often joined by the Secretary, a distinguished man named Esmond Butler, who had served as an assistant press secretary at Buckingham Palace prior to his arrival at Rideau Hall where he served as Secretary to six governors general for close to 28 years. Afternoon tea also included other members of the Household (all men) and the Governor General's military aides. Everyone was dressed appropriately, and two footmen served tea, tiny sandwiches and chocolate and maple éclairs, which everyone loved!

Dinners at Rideau Hall were always formal, regardless of whether there were many guests or just the Governor General and Mrs. Michener. The Micheners always dressed formally – black tie and long gown. Before the start of every dinner, there was a toast to Her Majesty the Queen. Two footmen, wearing white gloves and tailcoats, would stand directly behind them, at each end of the table. Conversations took place with their guests or between themselves when they were alone, but we were so focused on our work and on doing everything perfectly that we rarely heard what was being discussed. At the end of each course, Mrs. Michener would let us know, with a subtle nod, when it was time to clear the plates. This same formality was applied to all dinners, regardless of whether the vice-regal couple was in Residence at Rideau Hall, the Citadelle or on the train. Standards were exactly the same and never did we question them. It was part of our training and it had to be perfect each and every time.

During holidays and special celebrations, we also took care of Their Excellencies' families. Highchairs and jolly jumpers for the babies would be set up and the Residence was full of life. It didn't matter how many there were, this was their family home for five years and it had to be comfortable. At Christmas, trees were decorated, and all the rooms looked festive. Unfortunately, our own families had to take second place, but we never questioned this. We knew it was a part of our job and we were committed to making their time at Rideau Hall as memorable as possible. And for many of us, they often became like family.

Richard Legrand with President Mandela at Rideau Hall

The highlight of our week was Sunday evenings when dinner was served as a buffet so that the serving staff could have the evening off. We would set up the dining room with the food and Their Excellencies would serve themselves. Once finished, the Micheners loved to join us in the Ballroom for movie night! There was a projection room above the Ballroom from where a panel would open, and the projector would be ready to go. Every Friday, a chauffeur or orderly would drive to the old Nelson Theatre on Rideau Street to pick up a movie for the weekend. We made popcorn and served it in huge silver bowls! Mrs. Michener enjoyed those movie nights and always had treats for the staff. She particularly loved to pass around her Rogers' chocolates which were her favorite!

Saturday evenings were also fun because it was our bowling night. And, yes, there was a single bowling lane in the basement of Rideau Hall. To get to this secret spot, we had to go through the ladies' washroom in the basement and then through a single door to enter the bowling lane. Of course, because I was a rookie, I had to line up the pins. The older guys would throw those balls with a vengeance!

Sunday mornings were dreaded by the footmen! Mrs. Michener loved wearing hats, all kinds of hats, so she would often call up two or three of us to try on her hats while she decided which one to wear to church that day. It was difficult not to laugh while she changed the hats around until she was satisfied that she had the right one!

During our own meals or off hours, staff almost always gathered in their own dining areas. The footmen were called servants, the housekeepers were maids, and the kitchen staff were cooks. The cooks ate behind the kitchen, the housemaids ate upstairs, close to their sleeping quarters, and the footmen gathered in the basement. Even the dishes had distinct colours – blue, red, or green, with the crown stamped on all of them. Once they were washed, the dishes were returned to the "servants" areas.

The footmen's dining room was the largest, with a long wooden table covered with a red and white checkered cloth. It was there that we gathered in the evenings, sometimes including the aides-de-camp who would enjoy sitting with us and having a beer to talk about the day's events. It was also in this room where we could relax and be ourselves. The basement was for our staff only and the Governor General and Mrs. Michener respected our privacy. They were upstairs and we were downstairs and that was the way things were. Of course, this would change over the years as the number of staff increased, bedrooms were converted to offices and we no longer lived on site. But, until then, we were very much a family and, if something happened to one member of the staff, everyone felt it.

As I learned more about the workings of the Residence and about my role, the job no longer felt like work. Although working at Rideau Hall was not for everyone, I was determined to give it my best. Coming from humble beginnings, my family was proud of me and I felt it was a privilege to be there. It never entered my mind that things should be any different.

In 1996, Richard Legrand received the Royal Victorian Medal from Her Majesty The Queen for his service to the Office.

Maître d'Hôtel Richard Legrand in his office at Rideau Hall.
Photo credit: Bertrand Thibeault , Photographer

DUTY AND DEVOTION

"Once you walked through the swinging doors of the dining room, you were in a different world!"

Richard Legrand, Maître d'hôtel

After serving for 17 years as a footman at Rideau Hall, I was appointed Maître d'hôtel during Madame Sauvé's mandate. My predecessor, Jean Nadon, had been an excellent mentor for me but, for the most part, I learned by observing. I did not go to any special schools in London or Paris, but I was able to learn from good people. A certain "instinct" is an essential quality when working in a place like Rideau Hall. Not only is it an official Residence but it is also a place where history is made. Observing the moments, the events and the people is, without a doubt, a learning experience.

When I became maître d'hôtel, I was given carte blanche to do what I felt was necessary. With that, came the trust from my staff, my peers and my superiors. It was so important to me. I recall one day when Governor General Roméo LeBlanc asked me why we had so many plates on the tables for official dinners. He listened patiently to my explanation, pretending not to know the answer, and then replied "When I was young, we used to turn our plates over and eat dessert on the other side! But you clearly know what you are doing, so carry on. And besides, I don't think I can ask the President of France to turn his plate over for dessert!"

I also understood the importance of teamwork in an environment where expectations were high. Most of us had worked together for a number of years and my staff knew me well. With all that we did, whether it was for the Governor General, for dignitaries or for the public, there was no room for error. We needed to ensure that the unexpected never happened. Even as we set up tables in the Ballroom for official dinners, we would always check underneath to ensure that the table legs and mechanism holding the tables in place were secured so that the table would not collapse unexpectedly.

It was also important for me to be a mentor, to pass on what I had learned from those before me. I felt that, although traditions and protocol would change, the standards at Rideau Hall, for residents and guests, had to be the highest and the envy of similar institutions, both in Canada and around the world. On many occasions, we were told that our level of hospitality and service was unsurpassed.

I wasn't always easy on my staff. There were some difficult days and difficult decisions but I respected them and their loyalty. Their friendship was important to me. We were a family with the usual storms and battles, but I did my best to help them when they needed it and they, in turn, were there for me when I needed them. No matter what, I knew I could count on these guys and on their professionalism. They were devoted to their work, as were most of the staff members working behind the scenes at Rideau Hall. If there was a problem, guests never knew it. And "no" was never in our vocabulary.

Despite the increasing responsibilities over the years, my job at Rideau Hall remained the same – to serve the Governor General and to make the experience for everyone who entered through our doors to be as memorable as possible. My desire to serve was as strong as it was during my first weeks at Rideau Hall. Unfortunately, long days at a relentless pace do take a toll and my diagnosis of a chronic inflammatory joint disease developing in my spine made my decision to retire almost inevitable. Initially, I went through a range of emotions. Not only had I worked at Rideau Hall for almost four decades, but I had also lived in the Residence and on the grounds for most of my adult life. I was used to my personal plans always taking second place to the Governor General's plans and suddenly all this changed. I felt lost and unable to relax after so many years of handling details and decisions every day. For the first time, I felt that working in one place for such a long time might not have been a good thing.

Looking back now, I am grateful for the treasury of memories, mementos and experiences that will remain with me forever. More important, however, are the enduring friendships with those I served and those I worked with. They made the long days and countless hours worthwhile.

Richard Legrand, R.V.M., Maître d'hôtel

Tent Room at Rideau Hall prior to a formal dinner. From l to r: Footmen Peter Hannaford, Jimmy Carrière, Claude Lepage, Stuart Marc Tellier, Charles Proulx and Marc Boucher with Maître d'hôtel Richard Legrand.
Photo credit: Gene Hattori

GILLES (JIMMY) CARRIÈRE,
A LIFETIME OF SERVICE

I was 17 years old when I started working at Rideau Hall in 1965 during the Vanier mandate. I had just finished the 10th grade and was looking for work. My cousin was a footman at the Residence and told me that they were looking for a dishwasher. That same evening, a Friday night, I went straight to Rideau Hall to apply for the position. I was met at the side door by the chief steward who told me that, if I wanted the job, I needed to be there by 7:00 a.m. the next morning. Without hesitation, I gave up my grocery delivery job and prepared to start at Rideau Hall. I knew nothing about the Office or the Residence. I was just happy to work and the $15 a week, which included room and board, suited me fine. Could I have imagined that it was going to be the first day of an almost fifty-year career serving 10 governors general and their families? Not in a million years!

My name is Gilles but, when I first started at Rideau Hall, there was another employee also named Gilles – so my colleagues changed my name to Jimmy. The name came from the fact that, when we went to collect baggage from guests staying in the Residence, we would have to wear a white jacket and gloves. The white jacket made me look like a popular television series doctor from the 60s named Dr. James Kildare. The name stuck with me and, to this day, I'm still Jimmy to my former colleagues!

Back in the 60s, our staff was quite small, and we were very much like a family. Our duties were clearly defined, as were our living areas and sleeping quarters. There were four footmen, and our bedrooms were in the basement, along with a dining/sitting area where we would gather during off-hours. The housemaids (now called the housekeeping staff) had their spot on the third floor and the kitchen staff gathered in a room close to their work area. The maître d'hôtel, the head housekeeper, the valet and the dresser would eat together and, in the event of a royal visit, Her Majesty's valet and dresser would join them there. The footmen were not allowed in the kitchen so the pantry helpers (my title at the time) would bring the food to the different eating areas for the staff. Even the colours of the dishes were different for each group, so that the dishwashers knew where each set belonged.

The aides de camp were also not allowed in the kitchen, nor were they allowed to tell the footmen of any changes in meal requirements. They would have to speak to the Maître d' who would then convey the information to the respective groups. These clear divisions of both responsibility and position within the Residence made things much easier, particularly given the long hours and the fact that we all lived under one roof.

Menus were determined at a 10:00 a.m. daily meeting between Her Excellency and the Chef and Maître d'hôtel. The Maître d' would then share the menu with the footmen who would send the appropriate silver platters to the kitchen and the coffee and tea pots to the Steel Room via the dumbwaiter, a small elevator for carrying food and dishes between floors. The ladies who worked in the Steel Room (designated as such because of all the stainless steel in the small room) were responsible for preparing everything needed for the coffee and tea service, butter pats shaped as tiny maple leaves, sandwiches for daily high tea with members of the Household, and other similar duties.

Dinners were usually formal affairs, regardless of the number of guests. The aides were frequently used as "fillers" when a guest or two cancelled at the last minute (although this did not happen very often).

More often, if a guest or two were added, the Aide would be served his lunch on a tray in one of the sitting rooms, ensuring that he was always close by in case he was required in the Dining Room. Occasionally, when there weren't any official functions on the calendar, Mr. Vanier enjoyed eating his meal in his bedroom and the valet would take care of the service. Madame Vanier, on the other hand, loved to have dinner in the Dining Room and the aides de camp would be expected to join her, in black tie.

During the Vanier and Michener mandates, our uniform from June to October was a small grey waist coat, black livery pants, white tuxedo hard front shirt with studs and cuff links. We also had a hard collar that was added to the shirt as well as a cummerbund. From October to June, we wore the same kind of shirt with a vest with vertical white and black stripes and a heavy thick tailcoat with silver buttons. The livery pants were worn with suspenders and, with both uniforms, we wore white bowties which were eventually changed to black. For morning service, we wore a black suit with a long black tie.

During dinner, the senior footman would serve the wine and the footmen would serve the meal. They would then leave the Dining Room until the next course. Once all the courses had been served, the footmen would re-enter the Dining Room and stand at opposite corners of the room where they could be seen by the maître d'hôtel who would stand behind His Excellency. From there, he could face Her Excellency who would nod to signal to him that it was time to remove the dishes. In fact, the correct protocol was that Their Excellencies would wait for all their guests to finish their meal before taking their last bite. Once the nod came from Her Excellency, the maître d' would, in turn, nod to the footmen who would proceed with removing the dishes. Everything worked like clockwork and everyone knew their role.

For all events at Rideau Hall, regardless of size or when the last guest left, the unwritten rule was that all had to be cleaned up and put away. The next morning, the Residence looked like the event had never happened. There were long days and very early mornings. It was a lifestyle that came with the position and the responsibilities. We spent so much time at Rideau Hall that the staff became our family. We worked hard, never questioning the number of hours or days we were on duty. The staff was loyal and, for the most part, we enjoyed our work and were happy to be part of the group. Unfortunately, many of us did not see our children growing up nor were we there for important moments. It is my only regret.

Major change came about when, in 1966, the staff at Rideau Hall became part of the Public Service and part of a union which, unfortunately, did cause some problems. We worked in a Residence with a kitchen, footmen, housekeepers and office staff. We not only took care of the Governor General and his or her family, but we also took care of the guests. Our jobs were considered unique in the Public Service. Before the introduction of the union, we were paid by the week, regardless of the number of hours we worked. We did have a few perks, including that, once a month, we were allowed to order a 40oz bottle of liquor for 98 cents and a carton of cigarettes! When the union was introduced, the pantry helpers were paid $1.25 an hour and the footmen received $1.45. We were charged 60 cents a day for the "maid service" and 50 cents per meal.

Centennial year, 1967, was the most challenging for our staff at Rideau Hall. That year, with more than 60 incoming State visits from June to December, I worked for six months straight, 20-hour days, without a day off. The Queen and Prince Philip stayed at Rideau Hall for almost a week in late June and early July and we held many events to mark the Royal Visit and the Centennial celebrations. And, just a few hours after Her Majesty and His Royal Highness departed from

Rideau Hall, the President of Congo arrived. In addition to a large delegation, they brought with them a number of gifts and supplies, including many, many boxes of chocolate covered caterpillars which they generously shared with everyone, or rather, with anyone who was willing to try them. It certainly was a sharp contrast from the previous visit that week!

During my earlier years, many days and nights were spent on the vice-regal train, travelling across the country with governors general Vanier and Michener. The Ottawa train station during the Vanier mandate was in front of the Château Laurier hotel. If we were going to Toronto for an event, we would leave the Ottawa station at 11:30 at night and arrive in Toronto around 7:30 a.m. During the earlier trips, CN would hook up the vice-regal cars to the end of a freight train. It was slow and when we would round a bend, those cars sure were swinging! We went to Toronto so many times that I saw the CN Tower being built from the ground up.

When we travelled to other parts of the country, the train would stop in small towns and Their Excellencies would love to go outside to talk to the people from the area. It was a major event and most of the community was there to greet them. People would come all dressed up even if they were going to the train yards! The Micheners would often ask us to serve tea for guests on the station platforms and Mrs. Michener was always formally dressed, with her hat and gloves, while we served tea – silver trays and all. Quite often, if there were groups of school children present, the Governor General would give the students a day off from school, a gesture which was always acknowledged with loud cheers from the children and polite applause from the adults! A vice-regal visit was a big event in small town Canada!

While working on the trains, we were always paid 16 hours a day even though we often worked more. Regardless, at $18.00 a week, it was a good salary and a unique adventure. We had a front- row view of some of the most picturesque parts of our country! One time, I remember leaving Banff, Alberta to get to Vancouver. The Governor General, who had a few guests on the train with him, insisted on being awakened early so he could see the Rockies along the way. That day, we were up at 4:00 a.m. preparing breakfast which had to be served two rail cars away from the kitchen. Space was at a premium and, at one point, things got so crowded, we were sleeping next to the potatoes at the back of the kitchen rail car!

The vice regal train usually included two and eventually three private cars. The first car included His Excellency's office and bedroom, Her Excellency's bedroom, and a shared bathroom with a shower. The second car included a drawing room, a dining room with a table for up to 10 people, the Secretary's bedroom and a room with a table which, at the end of the day would convert to two bunk beds for the aides de camps. The third car included the kitchen and eating areas for the staff as well as a few small rooms for the valet, the dresser, the steward, the porter, the footman and a dishwasher. We had the smallest space, with a freezer between our beds next to the back door! It was an adventure, but we all enjoyed the journey.

Security at Rideau Hall was almost non-existent during my early years there. A tall black iron fence surrounded the perimeter of the grounds and one or two RCMP officers were usually on patrol. Occasionally, we would run into a visitor who had wandered into the Residence unnoticed or who wanted to meet the Queen but we were usually able to handle these incidents internally. One year, a major project to install a sprinkler system throughout the Residence was planned for the summer months. During this period, the Schreyers moved to the Mackenzie King Estate, the home of the former prime minister, in the Gatineau Hills. Every morning, a few staff members would travel to the Estate to bring food and necessary items for the family and we would return with anything that was not needed at the end of each day. During one of our return trips to Rideau Hall, we found that the gate near the entrance to the kitchen was locked. We needed to find the RCMP officer on duty to unlock the gate so that we could unload our truck and store the items we were bringing back to the kitchen. Unfortunately, we had no luck locating the officer on duty. Occasionally, the RCMP officers would cross the street to also patrol the Prime Minister's Residence at 24 Sussex. So, we decided to take matters into our own hands. I parked my truck very close to the locked gate that was near the kitchen and climbed the gate. I then managed to get through the unlocked window in the chef's office. My colleague helped by passing to me the material that needed to be stored and, when our task was complete, I climbed back out of the window, closed it and climbed back over the gate. We then left the grounds, without even being noticed by the RCMP!

Over the years, I was fortunate to have worked for so many great Canadians and served countless heads of state during their visit to Ottawa and to the Residence. I've had three private audiences with the Queen, who often spoke to me in French and thanked me for my many years of service. When the Prince of Wales came to Canada in 2014, my supervisor, Christine MacIntyre, singled me out and told His Royal Highness that I had been working at Rideau Hall for almost 50 years. Prince Charles appeared to be quite impressed with that level of loyalty and, at the end of his visit, he presented me with a tiny pillbox which he, himself, had painted.

In 1987, I was promoted from the position of Head Footman to Assistant Maître d'hôtel and, in 2000, I became the Maître d'hôtel, 35 years after my first day at Rideau Hall as a dishwasher.

I was once asked why I never showed any emotions while I was on the job. My reply was that I had a job to do and, regardless of how I felt or whether I agreed or disagreed, we were there to do the work. It was a philosophy that served me well.

Jimmy (Gilles) Carrière

Jimmy was awarded the Queen Elizabeth II Silver Jubilee Medal by the Rt. Hon. Jules Léger and the Queen's Golden Jubilee Medal by the Rt. Hon. Adrienne Clarkson, for outstanding service and dedication to the Office of the Secretary to the Governor General of Canada.

Assistant Maître d'hôtel Jimmy (Gilles) Carrière overseeing the dinner service in the Ballroom. Photo credit: Sgt Serge Gouin, Rideau Hall

TIPS AND TOES

One of the protocols we followed when serving wine at an official lunch or dinner was to pour the wine and then quietly back out of the room. This was easy for us since, as footmen, we did this almost daily… except for that one time when, as I was backing out of the room, Mrs. Schreyer, who was not supposed to be attending the dinner, unexpectedly walked in to say hello to the guests. Not knowing she was walking in as I was backing out, I stepped on her foot! I was horrified. Fortunately, no toes were broken and, equally important, not a drop of wine was spilled!

Gilles (Jimmy) Carrière, footman

Place setting with Rideau Hall state dinner china.
Photo credit: Gene Hattori

GARDEN PARTIES

Traditional Garden Parties, similar to those hosted by Her Majesty the Queen, were very much a part of the annual program at Rideau Hall and often signaled the unofficial start of the summer season. Until the 1980s, anyone who signed the guest book at the front of the Residence (visitors and VIPs) would receive a formal invitation to the Garden Party, regardless of where they lived. This meant that every spring, thousands and thousands of invitation cards had to be addressed by hand, even though the illegible handwriting on some of the signatures in the guest book reduced the load somewhat. Invitations were also sent to those on the official government list of precedence, which included high level officials and members of the diplomatic corps.

It was remarkable that people came from across the country for the Garden Party. They came with hats and gloves and fancy clothes and the event was similar to those held at Buckingham Palace, minus the Queen! Large white tents would be set up in the upper and lower terrace gardens with long skirted tables draped with pristine white tablecloths for tea, sandwiches and sweets served by the footmen who were impeccably dressed in black suits, crisp white shirts and bow ties.

The official start of the event was signaled by the arrival of Their Excellencies in the Upper Terrace Garden and the playing of "God save the Queen" and the Vice-Regal Salute by the Governor General's Footguards Band. According to protocol, food or drink service never started before the official anthems were played. Guests would then line up along stanchioned paths to shake hands with Their Excellencies before moving to the tents to enjoy hot tea served in china cups – never cold tea – with sandwiches and sweets. The sandwiches included tiny traditional cucumber sandwiches as well as egg and chicken salad, cut in triangles. An impressive array of cookies, tarts and squares filled the tables which were replenished by staff as supplies dwindled. All the food was made in our kitchens until the high volume made it impossible to store the food safely and eventually a catering company took over. The small square napkins with the gold-stamped vice-regal lion were abundant and often tucked away into a purse or jacket pocket as a souvenir of the event. About halfway through the afternoon, Their Excellencies would stop for tea and chat with a few visitors before resuming their handshaking in the receiving line. People waited patiently, while enjoying the sweet scent of the flowers and the background melodies. After almost two hours of shaking hands with the guests, Their Excellencies would return to the Upper Terrace where the playing of the national anthem would signal the end of the Garden Party for another year. Without a doubt, our Garden Parties were as elegant and enjoyable as those held in the royal gardens!

Like many things, time brings change and, somewhere in the mid 80s, it was felt that the Garden Party needed to be more inviting for younger crowds and families who, perhaps, would never otherwise visit the historic site. Newspaper, tv and radio ads replaced the formal invitations cards and the earlier Garden Parties, which were traditionally held in the private gardens were now spread out throughout the grounds. Hot tea was replaced by iced tea and fruit juices. Activities, performers, and popcorn tents were added to encourage younger families to attend. Attendance went from approximately 2,000 guests to almost 20,000 people! Visitors would line up outside the gates to be the first to come onto the grounds. At that point, I suspect that the free food and drink were perhaps more of a draw than the Governor General, but it was heartwarming to see so many people and children streaming through the gates. It was also not unusual to see the occasional guest with a shopping bag stocking up on sandwiches and treats but, for the most part, guests were there to enjoy the beautiful grounds. All staff, including family members, volunteered to help with the helium-filled balloons, handing out programs and serving the popcorn! By the end of the afternoon, the grounds cleared as quickly as they filled, particularly after the food tents closed. Staff sometimes worked twenty-hour days, but we had fun and, at the end of it all, it felt like we were welcoming these visitors to our own backyard. We wanted everything to be perfect and it always was!

Gilles (Jimmy) Carrière, Footman

Rideau Hall staff and family members often volunteered to help during Garden Parties that would draw well over 10,000 visitors to the grounds. L to r: Sylvie Barsalou, Alessandro Lappa, John Lappa and Luce Peterson.
Photo credit: Personal collection

MARION O'BRIEN, FROM HOUSEMAID TO HEAD HOUSEKEEPER

"Whatever I have, whatever I can do today, it is because of Rideau Hall. It was our home, and we were proud of it."

Marion O'Brien

I started working at Rideau Hall in June 1974, shortly after arriving from Jamaica. My mother had pushed for me to emigrate to Canada so that I could find a good job, maybe go to school, and have a better future. I, on the other hand, was reluctant to leave Jamaica because I had two small children and I didn't want to leave them behind. I finally agreed, knowing that it would be the best decision for my family. Was I scared when I arrived here? No, but I was lonesome. I was alone and knew no one. And I worried about my children.

When I arrived at the airport in Ottawa, I looked around but didn't see anyone waiting for me. I was told that the person who had sponsored me to be her housekeeper would be at the airport to meet me but, when no one came, I went to a ticket counter to see if someone could help me. It was only then that I learned, through the ticket agent who had contacted the sponsoring family, that the elderly woman I was hired to take care of had died, so the family no longer needed me. They claimed that they had informed the immigration office, but nobody told me this back in Jamaica. So many things were going through my mind, including what would I do next and where would I go. Fortunately, I was determined to give this new adventure a chance even though it wasn't easy.

I worked in a few places when I first arrived, from being a house-keeper and a babysitter for four little boys to cleaning rooms at the Holiday Inn. All the while, I continued to look for jobs at the employment office that I visited regularly. It was there that I learned of the opening for a housekeeper at 24 Sussex Drive, the Prime Minister's Residence. I had heard about Mr. Trudeau because he was a friend of the Jamaican prime minister, Michael Manley. The job was posted on a Friday but by Monday it was no longer available. The employment officer, sensing my disappointment, suggested that I go to Rideau Hall where there was also an opening for a housekeeper. I was reluctant because I really wanted to work for Pierre Trudeau, but I needed the job, so off I went, across the street, to 1 Sussex Drive.

When I arrived at Rideau Hall, I went right to the front door because, in Jamaica, that's what we do. I rang the doorbell. The footman who opened the door had a surprised look on his face when he saw me. I explained that I was there to see about a housemaid position, so he brought me to see Ms. Hermine Donner, the Head Housekeeper, who hired me on the spot because of my experience. That was 46 years ago, and it was then that my life in Canada truly began, with colleagues who would soon become my Rideau Hall family.

I lived in the Residence, like most of the other employees at the time. My bedroom was upstairs with the other housemaids and, even though our salary was not very high, we paid a very small amount for room and board. And our meals were always plentiful and good! The days were long, and we often worked "split shifts", starting at 7:00 a.m. and finishing around 1:00 p.m. Then we started again in the late afternoon and worked until about 8:00 p.m. We weren't paid for overtime work, but we could take time off when we were not too busy.

From the beginning, I liked my work. Rideau Hall was a beautiful Residence, full of history and tradition, and we had an important role to play in making the rooms as welcoming and warm as possible. The special guests who visited, including members of the royal family, were friendly with us and we wanted to make their stay memorable.

When I first met the Queen, we were lined up outside the royal suite to be introduced to Her Majesty so that she would recognize us if she required assistance. There were three of us and, upon being introduced to Her Majesty, the first two ladies tried to curtsy and almost dropped to the floor! When it was my turn, I had already decided that I was not going to curtsy because, I thought to myself, "she is the Queen, but she isn't God!" Her Majesty shook my hand with the biggest smile on her face. I'm sure she must have thought to herself "at least this one isn't going to drop to the floor!" And she never forgot me! Every time Queen Elizabeth comes to Rideau Hall, I see her, and she always brings me a little gift. I have a thimble, a little jewelry box, a wallet, a diary, and two picture frames from her. In fact, the last time Her Majesty gave me a frame, she smiled and said to me "You probably already have one of these!"

I recall one particular visit when we were rushing to prepare the Royal Suite just as Queen Elizabeth and Prince Philip were arriving on the grounds. Her Majesty was going to inspect the Guard and then they would enter the Residence to meet the Governor General's family and the Household staff. The Royal Suite had been prepared by two of the house-keepers and was ready for our special guests. However, just prior to the arrival, the RCMP went into the room with the security dogs and one of the dogs jumped onto the bed leaving paw prints on the bedspread. I went into the room for one final check and, seeing the marks, my heart almost stopped. I knew we always had two of the same items in case something needed to be replaced but, at that moment, I could not think of where the second bedspread was stored. I quickly removed the cover, took it down to wash off the marks and press it, and ran back up to replace the coverlet. The Queen's valet was in the room waiting for Her Majesty and, seeing the panicked look on my face, he quickly helped me to finish the bed just before the Queen arrived.

On another occasion, I was sitting in the cafeteria after a Garden Party, which was held at Rideau Hall in honour of Her Majesty. I was not working that day, so I was all dressed up to attend the outdoor event. After the Garden Party, I was in the basement having a cup of tea with some of the staff when one of the boys from the pantry came down to tell me that the Queen wanted to see me. I did not believe him because the "pantry boys" liked to play tricks on us, and us on them, so I kept drinking my cup of tea. Shortly after, he came back, this time with a more serious look on his face and said "Marion, Her Majesty is waiting for you!" When I realized he was serious, I jumped up and spilled the tea all over my dress. Fortunately, I had another fancy dress close by, so I quickly changed and ran up that grand staircase faster than I thought possible. Gracious as ever, Her Majesty simply wanted to present me with a little memento of appreciation. I was reminded many times afterwards that I was probably one of the few people in the world who had kept the Queen waiting!

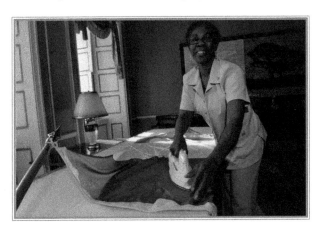

Marion O'Brien preparing the Residence for an incoming state visit.
Photo credit: MCpl Jean-François Néron, Rideau Hall

Another part of my job, which I loved, were the visits to the Citadelle in Québec. Their Excellencies would host and attend as many events as when they were at Rideau Hall. We were always busy. When it is time for Their Excellencies to return to Ottawa, the housekeeper is usually one of the last amongst the staff to leave the Citadelle, so that we can finish tidying up for next time. On this particular visit, it was the middle of February and I was supposed to leave at 8:00 a.m. the next morning with the chauffeur. That evening, I was alone finishing up in the private apartment, when I decided to take off my shoes so that I could be more comfortable while doing the cleaning. At the end of the hallway, there is a security door which is usually unlocked until we leave. This security door is between the Governor General's apartment and the apartment of the Commandant of the Royal 22ᵉ Régiment. It is a door which could be used as an exit in the event of an emergency or a fire and is always unlocked when Their Excellencies are in residence at the Citadelle. I would sometimes keep my cleaning products in this area behind the door, just to have them closer at hand. That evening, I opened the security door and went in to get something. I heard the door slam shut behind me and quickly discovered that it had been locked, probably by the RCMP, just after Their Excellencies left for Ottawa. I was locked in, with no shoes and no idea what to do. I knew the security guard would not check this little room, I did not have a phone and the driver who was supposed to pick me up the next morning would never think to look for me there. Fortunately, I quickly discovered that the security door on the side of the Commandant's Residence was still unlocked. I pushed open the door and entered the apartment, in my stocking feet. Surprisingly, I managed to find my way through the apartment to the front door, unnoticed! I did see a few warm coats hanging by the door and was tempted to take one but thought that would be too presumptuous, so I decided against it. I headed outdoors and took a run towards the front door of the Governor General's Residence which, in the best of times, might only be about 50 or 60 ft. away but, in February, and with the snow, it felt like it was much further. I started to bang on the front door, hoping that the security guard could hear me, but it was getting late, and it is a large Residence! I was worried and cold. Finally, after much banging, the guard came around and was shocked to see me standing there, in my stocking feet! Another one of my misadventures!

At times, staff had to be like security guards in the Residence. There were times when strangers or members of the public would find the front doors of the Residence open, so they would wander in. I recall one time when I was cleaning one of the rooms and saw a man wandering about. I asked if I could help him. He said that he wanted to have a talk with the Governor General. Right away, I alerted the RCMP. It was a different time, and it was not until the Sauvé mandate that the RCMP came to see Madame Sauvé about improving security on the grounds. Unfortunately, it took a number of incidents before everyone realized that security had been too lax in the past.

Over the years, I learned many things, both in my work and with the people I worked for. Most importantly, I learned to treat people with respect, regardless of their positions. And, in turn, I can honestly say that I was treated with respect, especially by the Governors General and their spouses. We would take care of them like they were our family – we looked after them and they looked after us.

When I first started at Rideau Hall, just months after I arrived from Jamaica, I never felt that I was discriminated against or that the staff resented me because I did not speak French. In fact, I will never forget Yves Chevrier, the Valet, who would chat with me as he was pressing clothes for the Governor General and he would try to teach me one French word every day. Yves and others like Richard Legrand who was a footman and later the maître d'hôtel at Rideau Hall, looked after me like I was a part of their family, something which meant so much to me as my own family was far away.

Miss Hermine Donner, who hired me and who was my boss for many years, was good to me even though she called me "the feisty one." She would often tell me that I probably wouldn't retire from Rideau Hall because, somewhere along the way, I would likely get fired because of my spunk, to which I hastily replied, "The only person I don't talk back to is my mother!" Despite my occasional "feistiness," Miss Donner was an excellent mentor for me and for others. Her expectations and her standards were high, and we all learned from her. She was very disciplined, and her eyes never missed even the smallest detail in the rooms. She taught us that things always had to be in their place and the rooms perfect at the end of each day, in case something happened in the middle of the night. The down-filled pillows were always plumped up and the Residence was always ready to receive guests 24 hours a day. It did not take me long to realize that, even though I came to Canada with a little knowledge about housekeeping, it was never as much as what I learned from my mentors and colleagues.

Over the years, I've had many ups and downs like everyone, and my Rideau Hall family was there for me throughout those difficult times. Many of the great Canadians I worked for, former Governors General and their spouses, have remained friends long after they left Rideau Hall. I will never forget when Governor General Roméo LeBlanc was about to leave, he told me to drop in if ever I was near his home in New Brunswick. He also told me not to bother calling beforehand because "there was always a pot of soup on the stove."

When we bid farewell to the families at the end of each mandate, it is difficult to say goodbye, but I always hope that I will see them again, and perhaps even share a few memories over a good bowl of soup!

Marion O'Brien began working at Rideau Hall as a Housemaid in 1974. She is now the Head Housekeeper, with more than 46 years of service to the Office. Photo credit: Sgt Serge Gouin, Rideau Hall

FLYING PILLOWS

One incident I will never forget occurred during a visit by the President of Brazil to Canada. The President, along with his delegation, was staying at Rideau Hall. Back then, every head of state visiting Canada stayed in the Residence and slept in the Royal Suite. The staff was proud to showcase the Residence and we went to great lengths to make their stay pleasant and memorable. In this case, I may have made the visit more memorable than planned.

While the President and members of the delegation were out of the bedrooms, the housekeepers cleaned and prepared the rooms for their return. I was in the Royal Suite making the bed when a gentleman came in, smiled at me and told me to go on with my work while he read the newspaper. I assumed that he was a member of the President's delegation or a security officer, so I went about my duties. At one point, the man dozed off and I forgot he was there. While making the bed, I took one of the pillows, meaning to throw it on the bed, and accidentally flung it at him! He was completely startled but not as much as I was when I discovered shortly thereafter that he was the President of Brazil!

Marion O'Brien, Housekeeper

Photo credit: Col Chris Weicker,
Rideau Hall

"As I approached the entry way of Rideau Hall, the front door opened before I even had the chance to turn the doorknob. There to greet me was a friendly face who said, "Welcome to Rideau Hall, please come in." It was as though the greeter knew the exact second when I would be arriving. As I entered the grand foyer of Her Majesty's official Canadian Residence, I knew that this was going to be a special morning."[6]

J. Byron Thomas

Front foyer of Rideau Hall with portraits of Governors General Michener, LeBlanc and Sauvé. Photo credit: Raymonde Chicoine Green

---

6   J. Byron Thomas, Canadian Monarchist News, Spring 2011, p.12

MARCEL SMIT, ORDERLY AND MORE

I recall that it was a cold but sunny day in November 1994, the kind of day that posed no problem for a major event, probably larger in size and scope than any which had ever been seen in small town Stellarton, Nova Scotia. A team from Rideau Hall had travelled to Stellarton to help with a special Bravery Awards ceremony which would end up being one of the most memorable events of my career. It was my job to ensure that the 180 men were lined up in alphabetical order, and to move them along when their names were called. Most were visibly nervous; others were emotional wrecks. Many wondered out loud why they were there. The medal for Bravery would be a solemn reminder of their role in the rescue operation of 26 of their fellow-miners in what was described as one of the most tragic mining disasters in Canadian history.

The Westray Mine explosion occurred on May 9th, 1992, in Pictou County, Nova Scotia, affecting the lives of most, if not all residents of that small community. Despite the risks, these men repeatedly went underground, regardless of unstable and dangerous conditions, searching for survivors and friends. Only 15 of the 26 bodies were recovered. As I watched the medal recipients that day, many of them younger than me, I thought of my own father who was a miner in the Netherlands and who had emigrated to Canada in June 1957 in search of a better life for his family. I was 15 months old when we arrived at Pier 21 in Halifax. Decades later, here I was in Nova Scotia again, playing a very small part in honouring these miners.

My first day at Rideau Hall was January 21, 1977 during the Rt. Hon. Jules Léger's mandate. I was hired as an orderly, a job which included anything that didn't fall within the range of other job descriptions at Rideau Hall. The title of "orderly" was carried over from the British regime and it came with the rank of honorary staff sergeant and a uniform – a red serge for formal events and the traditional green uniform for daily duties. It wasn't until I was about to start my new job that I began to question my ability to meet the challenges of the position. I was an Anglophone. I did not speak French and I was dyslexic. Regardless, I was determined to do my best. I soon realized that my position involved a lot of repetition so, when I made a mistake, I learned from it and didn't make the same mistake again.

I worked primarily in the mailroom with a supervisor named Don Desroches. There were only two of us who took care of a number of jobs. We worked in the basement, in a large room located directly below the Governor General's study. One of my primary responsibilities was to sort the mail and the daily newspapers and deliver them throughout the Residence. I also printed the next day's calendar of events, better known as the daily arrangements, on an 8x14 sheet that listed all the events on the Governor General's or the spouse's agenda for the following day. The arrangements also included the names of the aide-de-camp in-waiting, the anticipated numbers of guests attending the listed events, the appropriate dress code for the occasion etc. These pages contained the necessary details to inform the staff, including the chef, the valet and Her Excellency's dresser, of the comings and goings for the following day. I printed the daily arrangements with a Gestetner, a type of duplicating machine/printer which ruined many of my shirts because of the ink that needed to be loaded manually. When the secretaries or aides received the arrangements, they would cut out and tape the strips of paper with the details of the events in their bosses' daily planners as well as in their own. By the end of the year, these planners were full of strips of paper of different lengths and sizes protruding from the books, with the details of everything that happened each day that year. At the time and, lacking a better system, this was the most efficient way to maintain an accurate record of events without having to re-type complete pages of arrangements. When a last-minute change occurred, and they often did, we simply removed the strip of paper and replaced it with the corrected note. It was our version of today's "Outlook!"

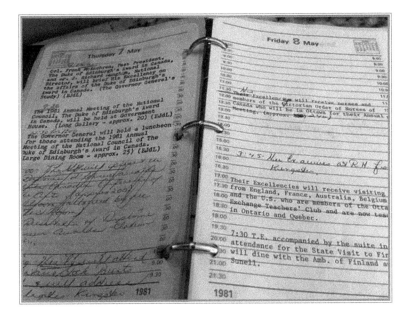

Daily arrangements for the Governor General's and the spousal programs were entered in diaries with a system that involved cutting strips of paper and taping them in the annual planners, until computers were introduced during the Sauvé mandate. Photo credit: Personal collection

Although my main responsibilities were in the mailroom and supplies office, a number of "other related duties" always seemed to land on my plate. As I learned to do them, I never for a moment thought that they weren't part of my job. For example, back in the late 70s, the Secretary to the Governor General, Mr. Esmond Butler, would regularly receive letters or messages from Buckingham Palace, written in code. When the messages came in, it meant taking out the large code book and decoding the message, which was usually about an upcoming visit or an appointment. Since I worked in the mail-room, someone decided to show me how to do the decoding to save time. With much persistence, I figured out how to decode and, at a minimum, I was able to provide a general idea of the content of the message for Mr. Butler's secretary, Miss Elizabeth Pitney, who would complete the work. However, it soon dawned on me that, here I was, decoding messages from Buckingham Palace when I did not even have my Canadian citizenship. I was a landed immigrant. Shortly thereafter, in 1979, I proudly became a Canadian citizen, at about the same time that modern technology did away with coded messages!

Another important part of my job was working at events which took place in the Residence. Dressed in my red serge, I would assist guests arriving or leaving and, although the occasional uninvited person would sometimes try to get into an event, for the most part, things went smoothly. That said, I did have a few close calls. One year, during the annual reception for the diplomatic corps, the chauffeurs for all the embassies were lined up outside the Residence with their limos, waiting for their ambassadors. When the ambassador from Iran was ready to leave, I called for his car. Unfortunately, I misunderstood and asked for Iraq's driver. Coincidentally, the ambassador of Iraq was also ready to leave just as the ambassador of Iran was about to get into Iraq's car. Fortunately, and thanks to the world of diplomacy, both gentlemen had a laugh and proceeded to their own cars. And I breathed a sigh of relief!

Marcel Smit at his post as Prime Minister Jean Chrétien and Mme Aline Chrétien arrive in the Ballroom. Background: Capt. Hercules Gosselin, Aide-de-Camp. Photo credit: Rideau Hall photographer

There were also those moments when the composure we are expected to maintain at all times gives way to stifled laughter or an unexpected reaction. One such event occurred when the Emperor and Empress of Japan were getting ready to depart Rideau Hall at the end of their visit. As they descended the front staircase, they shook hands and bid farewell to the staff gathered in the foyer. As usual, I was at my place near the front doors, fully dressed in red serge, which, over the years, had been adjusted to "grow with me". When the Emperor got to the front door, he shook my hand and, turning to the Empress said, "This is Mr. Sumo." Not only did we all laugh but I took the remark as a compliment since Sumo wrestlers are highly respected in Japan!

Things were not always as easy to control for large public events such as the Governor General's New Year's Levee, when I was always on duty and for long hours. I was responsible for counting the number of guests as they arrived, with a manual counter which I clicked for each guest. By the end of the day, when only staff was left behind, I would announce the number of guests we had received that day – often in the thousands. I always rounded up the numbers to the nearest hundred since I'm sure my fingers couldn't "click" as quickly as the guests arrived, especially at the start of the event. These were long days, but we all felt good about the end result and the days often ended with the staff gathering in the basement for a drink and a few good stories.

Some of our busiest days involved close to 18 hours of work. Events such as state visits, formal dinners, parliamentary evenings, investitures, and garden parties required many hours of setup and tear down time. Just before the event, everyone was at their posts, ready to receive the guests, almost like they were coming to our home. A number of us would remain in place until the last guest left and then the clean-up started. Everyone pitched in. When the lights went off at Rideau Hall, regardless of the time, everything in the Residence was clean and ready for the next day. It was our job to ensure that Rideau Hall was always at its best.

"When the lights went out at Rideau Hall, regardless of the time, everything in the Residence was clean and ready for the next day." Marcel Smit.
Photo credit: Rideau Hall photographer

Another one of my responsibilities was to ensure that the vice-regal flag was flying on the roof when the Governor General was in Residence. This protocol is still in place today and it is a way for the tour guides and visitors to know whether the Governor General is "at home." Unfortunately for me, the only way to access the flagpole on the roof would be to go up to the aides-de-camp's apartment which was located on the 3rd floor of the Residence. I would then go into their kitchen, pull down the ladder for access to the attic, climb up to the attic and then on to another ladder, which went up to the flagpole deck on the roof. I would then raise or lower the flag, mornings, evenings, and weekends, regardless of ice storms, wind, or rain. I became the flag guy!

During Her Majesty's visit for the Jubilee Year in 1977, I had to ensure that the Queen's flag was flying when she was at Rideau Hall. I was also asked to take a photo of the flag while it was flying above the Residence. Unfortunately, on that day, it happened to be extremely windy and I had to climb outside the safety barriers around the flagpole to get a good photo. All I could think of while I was up on that roof was the terrible newspaper headline the next day if something went wrong. I soon realized that I would have far more serious problems to worry about if something did, in fact, go wrong! Despite my concerns, the flag was flying, and the photo was taken, and I made it safely down the ladder and back into the aides-de-camp's kitchen! Eventually, the aides started offering to take care of the flags when I wasn't around, and they have continued to do so to this day.

When I first started at Rideau Hall, I thought that all the rooms were grand and more beautiful than anything I could have imagined. Rideau Hall was like a Canadian version of Buckingham Palace. A number of staff members lived on the grounds and it was very much a "working Residence". Unfortunately, the less visible rooms and offices in the basement were far from glamourous. In fact, parts of the basement were only timbers over dirt. Workplace safety seemed to be less of a concern back then and, although some of these areas were hazardous, any repairs or restoration would have involved a significant amount of work, time and dollars, which the Canadian taxpayer could hardly understand. The basement was eventually renovated but not until the Sauvé mandate when structural problems made it impossible to postpone the work any longer. Prior to the extensive renovations, there wasn't a cafeteria where the staff could purchase a meal or even buy a cup of coffee. With very few stores or restaurants close by, we were stuck if we didn't have a car or didn't bring our own lunch. In fact, one year, one of the maintenance workers set up his own little canteen in a hidden corner of the basement for staff to be able to purchase a few things. We had to go down through the basement, walk through the boiler room and make our way to "Armand's little underground canteen". Once there, he had a small hot plate and staff could purchase a can of soup, chips, chocolate bars and drinks. At one point, he even brought in a fryer and was making French fries – a real treat for the staff AND a real fire hazard! Obviously, rules were a lot different back then. The canteen lasted only until managers found out about it and quickly put Armand out of business! Not long after, a proper cafeteria for the staff was set up on the lower level.

During my time at Rideau Hall, I worked for eight Governors General. I started during the Léger mandate and both Mr. and Mrs. Léger were very special to me. Despite His Excellency's speech impediments after his stroke early in the mandate, he would often go around to the offices to speak with staff and to ask about their families. Madame Léger never left his side. We all felt like we were a part of their family, despite the formalities of their position.

Could I ever have imagined staying at Rideau Hall as long as I did? Probably not but it was not long after I started to work there that I realized how fortunate I was. My father passed away shortly after I arrived at Rideau Hall and the love and support I received from my colleagues confirmed that this was a unique and special place, and the staff members were very much like a family to me.

For those of us who were part of the everyday workings of Rideau Hall, it was obvious that life could be especially difficult for families living there. It drastically changed lives even if it was only for a few years. The whole Schreyer family, who came from Winnipeg, was uprooted to live in a big stone mansion, constantly surrounded by security and staff. Mr. Schreyer was the youngest Canadian appointed to the Office at the age of 42 and his four children were all quite young. I had a good relationship with the children – I was still young enough compared to some of the staff that had been working at Rideau Hall for many years. I will never forget seeing Lisa and Karmel, the two girls who were in their teens, sitting on the staircase together, looking so sad. They were in high school but probably felt like prisoners, constantly surrounded by security wherever they went.

The Schreyer children were pleasant and typically active, particularly the youngest, Toban, for whom the transition to Rideau Hall was probably the easiest. He was a cute little guy, and it was difficult for the staff to say no to him. Toban loved to play innocent tricks on some of us. I recall the time he had a small water pistol which he liked to aim at some of us in fun. One day, my boss, Don Desroches, and I were standing at the front door in red serge, waiting for guests to arrive for an event with the diplomatic corps. Toban was hiding behind a large pillar at the top of the stairs in the front foyer and called out, "Uncle Don, Uncle Don". When Don looked up and saw Toban with his water gun, he moved to avoid being the target and a spray of water went straight towards one of the guests, an ambassador no less! Fortunately, the person was wearing an overcoat and did not notice. I don't think I've ever seen a five-year-old move so quickly!

One thing that Mr. Schreyer used to enjoy was baseball games with the staff. He had a real passion for baseball, and I was told that, at one stage, he had to make a choice between being a professional baseball player and politics. During the summer months, our staff would rent the baseball diamond near Rideau Hall, and form two teams. Unfortunately, it was clear that the team that got the Governor General during the draw would win the game because he would hit that ball so far nobody could catch it!

The Schreyer mandate was a fun and interesting time at Rideau Hall. The quiet rooms of the Residence were often full of music and laughter and we were happy to see them happy and sad to see them sad. Mrs. Schreyer was good to the staff, always acknowledging special moments like birthdays or weddings.

I was fortunate to have been present for many memorable events, including royal visits and the visit of Pope John Paul II, when the Residence was filled with thousands of VIPs and guests. Our job was to ensure that everyone was lined up in order of precedence or with the groups they were representing. The receiving line started in the Ballroom and wound its way in and out of the many rooms at Rideau Hall, with His Holiness shaking hands with everyone along the way. There were over 1700 guests in the Residence that day and all went as planned and without a glitch, probably a testament to our dedicated staff and to lots of prayers!

In addition to the visits of world leaders such as Nelson Mandela, Lech Walesa, Ronald and Nancy Regan, and kings and queens from many countries, the most memorable and personally touching times for me were the visits of the members of the Dutch Royal family. I was fortunate to have met Queen Juliana, Queen Beatrix, Princess Margriet and, more recently, King Wilhelm Alexander who visited Canada in 2015. As usual, I was helping with the tree-planting ceremony that always takes place on the grounds of the Residence during a state visit. This time, however, a long-time colleague and today the Executive Director of Events, Household and Visitor Services, Christine MacIntyre, arranged for me to meet King Wilhelm following the ceremony. I was so proud to speak with him in Dutch and he was clearly pleased to hear of my own role at Rideau Hall. Later, as we were preparing for the state dinner that evening, I was invited to join one of the tables in the ballroom because of a last-minute cancellation. I could not have been prouder.

The visit of Terry Fox to Rideau Hall is also one that remains among my most treasured memories. The day of Terry's stop in Ottawa, the event coordinator had invited approximately 200 school children to come to Rideau Hall to greet him when he arrived. Terry ran up the main drive of the Residence and was welcomed by Mr. Schreyer and the children. Afterwards, they all moved into the Ballroom and Terry spoke to the children, inspiring them to work towards their dreams. He then bid farewell and left for the next part of his journey in Ontario. Unfortunately, it was never completed.

Over the years, my position at Rideau Hall evolved. Some of my earlier jobs such as "orderly" disappeared, others were replaced with technology. The number of staff members increased, and job descriptions were more clearly defined. That said, when someone needed to find something, fix something or explain something, I was often the person they turned to. After so many years, Rideau Hall had become a second home for me, and I had come to know all or most of its nooks and crannies. Even the Governor General would call me directly if he or she was looking for something. As always, I would do my best to get answers or help find solutions.

The uniqueness of working at Rideau Hall is also part of the challenge at times. The timeline for each new mandate includes a period of adjustment when the new Governor General and his or her family arrive, often a nervous time for them and for the staff. We all want to make the transition from their home to "the big house" as comfortable as possible, but it never comes without bumps along the way, especially if there are children involved. For the permanent staff, the repeating pattern then starts – from the anxiety of starting over with a new "boss" every five or so years, to adapting to the pace and demands of each new mandate and, finally, to the build-up of emotions as the Governor General and his or her family begin to prepare for the transition back to "real life". It was not unusual for those of us who witnessed many transitions to sometimes have that feeling of déjà vu. Fortunately, I learned early on that flexibility and patience were essential qualities for my position and, in fact, for most positions at Rideau Hall. Every day was unique and almost every day brought a new story for the memory books!

Marcel Smit, 38 years of service

Marcel Smit received the Queen Elizabeth II Golden and Diamond Jubilee Medals as well as the Vice Regal Commendation for long-term and outstanding service to the Office of the Governor General.
Photo credit: Rideau Hall photographer

SENSE AND SOUVENIRS

It was not unusual for guests to leave Rideau Hall or the Citadelle, particularly after formal events, with "unauthorized souvenirs". Sometimes we spotted them and, other times, the oversight was brought to our attention by a senior member of the Household who would watch to see how we "rescued" the item from the guest. With the utmost discretion, we would politely remind the guest that they had forgotten to return the spoon or the dessert plate to the table before leaving the room. Sometimes, we succeeded. Other times, we watched as the item was slipped into a jacket or purse and walked out of the Residence with its new owner. My most challenging time with a guest was when I had to remind him that he would have to leave the fine bottle of scotch at the bar, before departing. He looked at me with complete indignation and replied, "oh come on, I pay my taxes!" Enough said.

Marcel Smit

"As footmen, we never knew who would come through those front doors or who would be staying in our guest rooms. From Her Majesty the Queen to Céline Dion, Wayne Gretzky or Leonard Cohen… we knew what we had to do, and we just did it."

Tim Roberge, Head Footman

TIM ROBERGE, HEAD FOOTMAN

I was 17 when I started working part-time at Rideau Hall as a dishwasher. I was still in high school and I would go to work when they needed me, mostly for large events and dinners. I really didn't mind the work, and it eventually led to a full-time job. Never could I have imagined staying there for more than 40 years. More importantly, I could never have imagined the interesting times I witnessed, the experience I gained and the amazing people I met during those years.

Rideau Hall is a residence. It is not a hotel nor is it a banquet hall. The guests can be world leaders, members of a royal family or everyday Canadians. To us, they are all VIPs. The temporary residents, namely the Governor General and his or her family, are also VIPs, but, unlike the guests, the next five or so years launch them into a world of busy schedules, with high security details and staff members who are at their service 24 hours a day. It is a period of adjustment for everyone and, for those of us who have worked at Rideau Hall for so many years, we do our best to ensure that the experience for the new residents is as positive and pleasant as possible. The staff genuinely want them to be comfortable in their new home. At the same time, we realize that it cannot always be easy.

It was during the Schreyer mandate that I became a full-time employee at Rideau Hall. School was behind me and I had watched and learned a lot from those working around me, mostly footmen and kitchen staff. I enjoyed watching the events unfold from behind the scenes – everyone had a role, and everyone had their place in the execution of an event. In 1999, during the Clarkson mandate, a permanent position became available (which didn't happen very often) and I became a footman. I began wearing the traditional uniform, a dark suit and tie and, even though I was still the same guy, I felt that everyone looked at me differently. I was proud to be a footman and, 18 years later, I was appointed to the position of head footman.

I am often asked about the changes that have occurred at Rideau Hall since my earlier years. Some traditions have withstood the test of time, others have changed to reflect more current trends, and some have been left by the wayside. We still polish silver by hand to protect the finish, but we no longer use as many pieces as often as we used to. Some of these pieces date back to the 1800s and many were gifts from the royal family or heads of state. Polishing the silver was one of my many duties and I will never forget, during my earlier years, when I had a handful of knives with silver handles which needed to be cleaned. Since we could not use any abrasive pads on the silverware, I placed the knives in a glass container filled with the silver cleaner and put them in the cupboard to soak. A few days later, I remembered that I had left the knives in the container and, in a panic, I went to retrieve them. The acid from the cleaner had eroded all the metal! And the knives had to be discreetly thrown out!

As for the silver candelabras that graced the elegantly dressed tables at each dinner, Governor General LeBlanc decided that they were preventing him from seeing the guests sitting across the table, so they were replaced with beautiful floral arrangements adorned with tea lights. Unfortunately, those tea lights can pose their own hazards. Just before an Order of Canada dinner, as we were about to open the doors into the magnificent Ballroom for the guests to be escorted to their seats, one of the footmen noticed flames shooting up from the center of a table. One of the menu cards that was placed at each setting had fallen onto a tea light. Within seconds, it caught fire and created quite the flame. Fortunately, we were able to extinguish it before the sprinkler system in the Ballroom became activated. Except for a slight scent of smoke, the guests remained dry and the evening was perfect as always!

Polishing silver is one of the responsibilities of the footmen at Rideau Hall. Tim Roberge, now Head Footman, has worked at Rideau Hall for more than 40 years. Photo credit: Rideau Hall photographer

During the Clarkson mandate, much emphasis was placed on showcasing Canadian products and specialties from different regions. The chef spent hours writing up menus for special events which were then approved by Their Excellencies. Our menus often read like a culinary class and a geography lesson at the same time. Madame Clarkson and Mr. Saul knew a great deal about Canadian food and wine, and they encouraged creativity in the kitchens. It was also important to them that the footmen and the staff members hosting each table knew what was being served so that they could answer all or most questions from the guests during dinner. In fact, each table host was provided in advance with tiny "cheat sheets" which included interesting notes or details about the guests at their table, including their profession, interests, hobbies etc. The amount of preparation that went into a dinner went far beyond the menu.

The cheese service, which came after the main course and at the same time as the salad, was particularly important. We had to go around to each guest and explain the names of the cheeses on our tray, where the product came from and the type of cheese it was. Sometimes, the different cheeses were even placed in geographic order on the serving tray, making it easier for us to memorize the script! Occasionally, when a new cheese was introduced, we would forget the name or the place of origin or some other detail. That was when we had to be creative and hope that the noise level and the wine were enough to muffle our descriptions!

One time, during a small VIP dinner, I was serving a fairly well-known former politician who listened to my explanations about the cheeses and stopped me to say that one of the cheeses on the plate originated from Sir Wilfred Laurier's hometown. "But of course, that is way before your time," he said to me. Without hesitation, I replied "actually Sir, I went to his high school!" It caught him off guard and I even surprised myself with my spontaneous reply which, fortunately, added some levity to the evening. And then there was the time when one of the guests took the knife from one of the softer cheeses, placed a chunk on her plate, licked the knife like a popsicle, and put the knife back on the tray! Without hesitation, I walked into the kitchen, changed my tray and utensils and continued the service.

One of the more interesting but also more "physical" jobs of a footman is serving the guests during formal dinners. In the past, it was traditional to serve plated meals where individual portions were brought to the tables, each covered with a silver "cloche", a sort of dome covering each plate. With a nod from the maître d'hôtel, the domes were removed simultaneously to reveal the main course. This type of service was changed in more recent years so that the footmen would move around to each guest, presenting the main course with sides on a large silver platter, along with a serving fork and spoon.

Guests would serve themselves from the platter and the footman would then move on to the next guest. A second footman would follow with gravies or sauces. Of course, a heavy silver tray filled with food can require some balancing skills to avoid the guests wearing their dinner! One special guest summed it all up for me and for those seated at his table that evening. It was a black-tie dinner which follows all the Order of Canada ceremonies and I was walking around the table holding the large serving platter and stopping at each place to help the guests serve themselves. Mr. Paul Anka, one of our greatest singers and songwriters, had received the Order of Canada at an earlier ceremony and was a guest at the table I was serving. As I leaned in close to him with the tray, he commented on how heavy the silver platter must be. I replied, "It is. I just don't want to touch your shoulder with it." He laughed and started singing "Put Your Head on My Shoulder...", one of his most famous songs. The table burst out in laughter and there I stood.... while Paul Anka sang to me!

Tim Roberge serving during a black-tie dinner which traditionally follows Order of Canada investitures. Photo credit: Rideau Hall photographer

Less entertaining but equally memorable was the time I was serving the head table for a state dinner. State dinners are the most formal of our events and the scenarios are usually dictated by protocol and diplomacy, along with countless meetings between officials from both countries. Again, the main course was being served on a large oval platter which, that evening, included small Cornish hens. The President was wearing the full national dress from his country, covered from head to toe in silk and gold trim. Following the proper protocol, I was to serve the President first and then the Governor General. The President looked a bit puzzled but proceeded to take some vegetables from the platter. He then reached for the Cornish hen which, unfortunately, fell directly onto his lap and then onto the floor. To make matter worse, the President's napkin was not on his lap so all I could see was the stain from the Cornish hen on the silk tunic. Never, in all my years, had this happened to me! The President tried to hide his embarrassment by acting as if nothing had happened, as did I! I proceeded directly to the kitchen to fetch another hen and, when I returned a few moments later, I noticed that the napkin was now on the President's lap and the original Cornish hen had been discreetly kicked under the table.

One of my moments of fame at Rideau Hall was in a story which Governor General David Johnston told Prince William during his visit to Canada in 2011. Early in the Johnston mandate, Their Excellencies were hosting a black-tie dinner for the Aga Khan. After the dinner had ended and the guests had left, His Excellency went upstairs to their private apartment so that he could take his dog Kato out for a walk on the grounds, something which he would often do in the evenings. Unfortunately, that evening, Kato decided to take on the local neighborhood skunk! And, unfortunately for me, I happened to be the first person that His Excellency encountered as he came through the side door from the gardens! I ended up spending the next little while in the shower of the private apartment, with the Governor General, washing down Kato with tomato juice. So, a couple of years later, when our team of footmen was being introduced to Prince William and Princess Kate, Mr. Johnston stopped and told the Prince about the time he and I were in the shower dealing with a skunk attack! I've heard the story recounted several times by Mr. Johnston and, many times during his speeches, he would pause to see if I was in the room to confirm that the story was indeed true! For that reason, I thought it was most appropriate for me to present Mr. Johnston with a parting gift on the last day of the mandate, just prior to his departure from Rideau Hall – a bottle of "Skunk Off" – because there won't always be a footman around to help clean the dog!

In the more than 40 years I have worked at Rideau Hall, and more specifically, since becoming a footman, I have served at every Order of Canada investiture dinner, state dinner and countless events in between. I can't deny that those earlier years washing dishes and helping in the pantry were a part of my training, but I learned the most from a team of individuals who were proud of the work they did and who knew that they were representing the Office and what it stood for. We all knew what we had to do, and we just did it whether we were working for 18 hours straight, seven days a week, or just serving the family dinner and feeling like we were a small part of their world.

I am often asked how I have been able to stay in one place for so many years. For most of us, working at Rideau Hall is like having a new job every five years. Every Governor General is different and every one of them brings an expertise and expectation that defines the mandate. In each case, flexibility is the key to welcoming and accommodating the temporary residents. And even though there is always a tear at the end of a mandate, we know that our jobs must be done so that they can do theirs.

Tim Roberge

Tim Roberge, Head Footman, 42 years of service to Rideau Hall
Photo credit: Rideau Hall photographer

KINDRED SPIRITS

For as long as I've been at Rideau Hall, there have been rumours about the building being haunted. The stories often refer to an eerie presence, a single spirit that roams the halls or shows up in the dining room, sitting at the end of the beautiful long wooden table. A number of individuals I've worked with would avoid that part of the Residence at night because of unexplained occurrences. In fact, a security officer I know left suddenly one evening, claiming to have seen a white silhouette sitting at the table when he was doing his rounds. He never returned to Rideau Hall.

I will never forget my own encounter with the ghost of Rideau Hall. My shift that day was 12 to 9 p.m. I finished serving dinner at 8:00 p.m. and I then had to prepare two rooms on the second floor, for guests who were to arrive at Rideau Hall later that evening for an overnight stay. As is customary before overnight guests arrive, I checked both rooms to make sure all was in order, closed the doors and returned a short time later with a fruit basket, a plate of cookies and a bucket of ice for each room. I went first into the Vanier room which looked over the gardens behind the Residence. I placed the items on the table and closed the door. I then crossed the hall and headed towards the Aberdeen room. My hands were full as I juggled the basket of fruit, the cookies and the ice. Suddenly, the door started to open as if someone was on the other side. I know there wasn't a draft which would have caused it to open and no one else was working that evening. As I entered the room and looked around, I remember feeling an unnerving presence, but there was no one there but me. Perhaps it was my imagination playing tricks on me, so I quickly settled the items I had to place in the room and turned to leave. As I closed the door the door behind me, I whispered "thank you" in the hope that, if anyone was watching, he or she might consider me a friend. Just in case…

Tim Roberge, Footman and vice-regal ghostbuster

Dining Room. Missing from photo: The ghost of Rideau Hall.
Photo credit: Rideau Hall photographer

INSIDE THE BIG HOUSE

"I think traditions have meaning and should be respected. The Crown represents everything that is stable in our society, and as the representative of the Crown in Canada, the Governor General has an obligation to make sure that the respected institutions continue to be meaningful."

The Rt. Hon. Adrienne Clarkson

The Rt. Hon. Adrienne Clarkson, *Heart Matters*, Penguin Group, Toronto, 2006 p. 195

THE CRÈME DE LA CRÈME

There are two, unforgettable, and alarming days for Governors General and their families: the day they arrive at Rideau Hall, and the day they leave. The 26 briefing books we were given prior to my husband taking Office did not even come close to preparing us for what lay ahead.

We returned to the "big house" from the Installation ceremony at the Senate on February 8th, 1995, and walked, bewildered, into the Ballroom to a sea of approximately 165 unfamiliar faces assembled to welcome us. This was the staff. Almost five years later, on October 9th, 1999, we trod the slow farewell march towards the front door, flanked on both sides of the main corridor by most of these same people. Now they had become family. On the way to the train station to take the overnight sleeper to Moncton, we could not say a word to each other for the lump in our throats.

At the beginning of the mandate, job descriptions such as: footman, aide-de-camp, chief herald, commissionaire, valet, and camériste were a mystery yet-to-be discovered. There were so many different departments – pods of excellence – that I despaired of ever knowing who they were, or where they were located. It would be impossible to name each person who helped us remain reasonably sane and productive during what we thought would be an eternity, but which turned out to be over in a flash.

There were, in no special order: the senior staff holding and preserving the corporate memory; the press office and photographers; the aides-de-camps; the correspondence unit; the event planners; the housekeeping team; the kitchen and pantry crews; the secretarial and administrative staff; the chancellery personnel; the translators; the drivers; the mail room and records team; the IT department; human resources and finance; our well-trained tour guides and the exempt staff (though I never did find out what they were exempt from!) Although not part of the in-house staff, other essential guardians of our wellbeing added to our security, and to the beauty and serenity of our surroundings: gardeners who maintained the 79 acres; RCMP officers and commissionaires; Canadian Forces musicians invited to play at all the official functions; ceremonial guards steadfastly on sentry duty at the front gate, who also performed the Changing of the Guard ceremony on Parliament Hill.

I often felt we were actively participating in an exquisitely choreographed performance lasting nearly five years. The warmth and hospitality provided inside Rideau Hall during an event such as the Order of Canada investitures were unsurpassed from the moment the front doors opened until the very last guest left. There was always a magic moment during formal dinners, for instance, when the maître d'hôtel, Richard Legrand, gave the signal for the mirrored doors of the ballroom to open and, simultaneously, all the footmen would enter bearing platters and shining domes of culinary masterpieces lovingly prepared by chef Jacques Parent and his team. It was like a mixture of scenes from the Nutcracker Suite and chapters from Charles Dickens' Christmas Carol, and I never tired of seeing the pageant repeated. There were other memorable vignettes from those years: Marion, the housekeeper, wagging her finger of disapproval when she felt people were not living up to her standards (myself included); our wonderful three drivers: Jacques, Ghislain, and Patrick about whom I could write a full book; and Gabrielle Lappa, one of the first people we met and the last person we said goodbye to. She was always a voice of reason and kindness.

I have left to the last two special people who worked tirelessly behind the scenes for us on a daily basis, both at the Residence and while we were travelling. Without them, we would definitely not have survived the mandate. We leant on them heavily for their assistance, their knowledge, and their wisdom, but we also valued their discretion and loyalty both to the institution and to the vice regal families they looked after. They became our intimate confidants, which must at times have been a heavy burden on them, while always remaining professional and respectful. We knew that, somehow, they would manage to see us successfully through each ordeal, and they did.

In his early twenties, Yves Chevrier became valet to former Governor General Vanier, and went on to serve eight successive governors general by the time he retired 51 years later. My husband and Yves had the most gentle and amicable relationship, greeting each day with the same ritual of orange juice and pleasantries. Their favourite activity was going to the auction together, usually once a month, sitting in the front row, with Yves doing the bidding for all manner of bric-à-brac, most of which we did not need.

Very soon after the start of the mandate, Lucie Lortie became my dresser. She had been Madame Sauvé's dresser in the early 1980s, so she was well versed in the requirements and demands of vice-regal life. From Québec, Lucie was beautiful, chic, poised, and very funny. I am sure she had no intention of taking the position but came to the interview out of courtesy. I was still trying to finish my degree in social work at McGill and had another year to go before graduating. Lucie must have sensed how desperately I needed help with everything: hair, make-up, wardrobe, the routines and conventions of the Office. Much to my relief, she agreed to take the job. Our schedule of events was extremely heavy, especially on state visits, and I remember one such gruelling trip to India when I had nine different events in one day as the temperature soared to over 100 degrees. Lucie managed to get me impeccably groomed, changed and on time, nine times!

I know that I speak for Roméo as well when I say that no words can ever truly convey our gratitude for the help, advice, and affection that we valued so much from such a professional and devoted group of hard-working people. They went way beyond the obligations of duty. They were truly the "crème de la crème."

Diana Fowler LeBlanc, C.C.

President Mandela, accompanied by the Rt. Hon. Roméo Leblanc at Rideau Hall. In the background are (l to r) Diana Fowler LeBlanc, JoAnn MacKenzie, Director of Finance and Gabrielle Lappa.
Photo credit: Rideau Hall Photographer

A NEW ENERGY AT RIDEAU HALL

In 1979, the Right Honourable Edward Schreyer became, at the age of 42, the youngest Canadian Governor General. Mr. Schreyer's wife, Lilly, was an active woman, determined to make life at Rideau Hall as normal as possible for their four children who ranged in ages from 4 to 13, with the youngest being little Toban.

The Schreyer mandate brought with it a certain amount of energy which comes with having four young children and teens in the house! Although protocol and traditions were still very much respected, routines did change for all of us so that the children could enjoy as normal a life as possible in the big house! Very little changed on the public side of Rideau Hall but, behind the scenes, we all adapted to this new normal! Meals in the private quarters consisted of simpler menus and we learned that macaroni and cheese and hot dogs could be made to look quite elegant on silver platters! I know that the chef was slightly miffed when he was asked to make grilled cheese sandwiches for lunches. We didn't think our French chef even knew what a grilled cheese sandwich was, but he learned quickly when we explained that it was a "simpler version" of a "'croque monsieur", minus the meat!

The newly modified private quarters accommodated the young family as well as "Auntie Martha", a family friend and nanny who had come from Manitoba with the Schreyers to help with the children. She was definitely busy, as the Schreyers had a very full program, but we all helped and eventually Rideau Hall became their home. There certainly were times when we had to politely chase the kids and their friends out of the state rooms, particularly when they were on their skateboards!

Reggie, the Irish setter family pet, was also quite comfortable in all the rooms and occasionally left his mark to prove it! The Residence was full of life, and school friends came and went. Our staff did what we could to make Rideau Hall their home and, as time passed and the children grew older, it was like they were our own. We were always looking out for them.

Mr. Schreyer was always pleasant. He was an avid reader who could spend hours in his study reviewing material or discussing the topics at hand. Mrs. Schreyer, on the other hand, was a lively, beautiful woman. Although most of their summers were spent in Lower Fort Garry in Manitoba because the Citadelle was being rebuilt after the fire, the Schreyers did spend some time in Québec during the reconstruction period. Unfortunately, the Citadelle is a military fortress and it does come with challenges if one wishes to have some privacy or leave unnoticed, particularly when the RCMP is responsible for the security detail of the vice-regal family. Which is why a few of the footmen agreed to help Mrs. Schreyer to "escape" on her own occasionally. This did not happen often but when Her Excellency wanted to go shopping or for a long walk in the city, we would take her down to our secret passageway which was in the basement of the fortress. There, we had discovered an old wooden door which opened onto a narrow dirt pathway leading to the famous Dufferin Terrace in the old historic part of Québec. Unfortunately, a deep trench separated the pathway from the terrace. So, in order to access the Terrace, we had devised our own "drawbridge" by sliding the top of an 8^{ft} table across the trench and we could then cross over to the Dufferin Terrace and leave the Residence unnoticed. Our escape route worked perfectly. I must admit that I was always a bit nervous about using it, especially for Mrs. Schreyer, but we were always there to help her walk across the table and onto the footpath. She would then continue on her way, wearing her headscarf and sunglasses, to enjoy the city as any visitor or tourist would. Mrs.

Schreyer would give us an approximate return time so there were always two footmen waiting at the basement door to push the tabletop back across the ridge and escort Her Excellency back into the Residence. I must admit that it worked well as long as there was always someone there to pull back the tabletop and store it, thus preventing anyone from entering the Residence from the outside!

Our little secret worked well for a couple of years until, one day, the security officer came looking for Mrs. Schreyer! Someone found out about the "escape route" and we were in trouble! We went down to the basement and had to disclose our secret to the RCMP! Needless to say, a few people were not happy about the new restrictions which were imposed when the security officers installed barbed wire around the back perimeter of the Residence to prevent anyone from getting into the Residence ...or out!

Having the Schreyers at Rideau Hall was very different from previous mandates. For our team, it was five years of high energy in what was previously a very quiet house! It must not have been easy for the young occupants but, eventually, we became a part of their extended family. Five years later, it was once again time to move on, sometimes the most difficult part of our job.

Richard Legrand, Footman

The Schreyer family brought new energy to Rideau Hall. (1979-1984)

LE CHEF DES CHEFS

I was first introduced to the world of cooking when my dad, recognizing that I had an interest in the profession, encouraged me to go to an interview for an apprenticeship position at the old Monastery of the Dominican Fathers on Empress Street in Ottawa. Chef Lucien Bergeron, a well-known Ottawa chef at the time, was moving on from his position at the monastery and they were looking for a young apprentice to assist the new chef. I was 17 years old and daily life in a monastery was as new to me as life at Rideau Hall! Fortunately, my father accompanied me to the interview or I might have turned back and never have known the path that was laid out for me that day.

Our meeting at the monastery was with the new chef and the senior priest. Following a brief discussion, I was hired and told to start the next day. My father, who had come from a traditional Catholic family of 11 boys from Grondin, Quebec, was happy for me, recognizing that this opportunity could lead to others. And it did. During those first six months, I learned the basics of working in a kitchen under the young chef who, to me, seemed to know everything. After several months, Chef Bergeron decided to return to the monastery and things changed significantly. Not only was he set in his ways, but his ways included teaching me the culture and the "unwritten rules" of a kitchen. There were times when he reduced me to tears because he was so demanding. It took awhile but I eventually recognized that he was pushing me to do better. Following my experience at the monastery and my completion of the Professional Chef Program at Algonquin College, I continued my apprenticeship at the National Arts Centre under the tutelage of highly respected Executive Chef Kurt Waldele who soon became my mentor. It was during that time that I was introduced to fine cuisine on a grand scale and that I witnessed, with admiration, the collaboration of Rideau Hall Executive Chef Stephen Gervais and Chef Kurt on special events. I knew then that the greatest kitchen in the country was at Rideau Hall.

To work as an executive chef, in any capacity, is a privilege. When I first arrived at Rideau Hall as a sous-chef, I was inspired, not only by the surroundings and the people I worked with, but also by the people we were cooking for. Whether it was for the Governor General and his or her family, members of the royal family, dignitaries from around the world or Canadians from all walks of life, the inspiration and the effort were the same.

Each year, there are, on average, 400 events in the Governor General's or the spousal calendar, at Rideau Hall or la Citadelle. Planning for each event is multi-faceted and involves numerous players who have a key role in the success of each event. Like any workplace, working at Rideau Hall can present challenges. Long days, 80 hours+ work weeks and ever-changing decisions are expected. We are responsible for all meals for the vice-regal family in addition to planning, managing and stocking the kitchen for official events as well as for the staff cafeteria. As is the case for every section within the Residence, it does take some time before personal tastes are known and before we are able to master the "favorite comfort foods" of our primary clients—the vice-regal family. In our world, we are trained to be perfectionists so, at times, it can be difficult accepting that we will not always be preparing Michelin star menus, even though we welcome the challenge! And, as in most homes, there are some recipes that are anchored in time, such as the shortbread cookies which likely date back to the late 1800s and the days of Lord and Lady Aberdeen who, in their role as the vice-regal couple, might have transported the recipe from the United Kingdom!

In more recent years, Rideau Hall has excelled in its ability to showcase all things Canadian. From the food and wines of all regions of the country to the arts and accomplishments of Canadians, the Residence is truly Canada's House. Just as the Rt. Hon. Roméo LeBlanc enjoyed seeing his Acadian specialties served to our guests, our menus today feature unique seasonal ingredients and recipes from coast to coast to coast.

Chef Louis Charest and his team preparing for an official dinner. From l to r – Chef José Moniz, Chef Simon Martin, Chef Gilles Lepage and Executive Chef Louis Charest. Credit: Ronald Duchesne, Rideau Hall photographer

I am often asked about the favorite meal I have prepared at Rideau Hall. Without hesitation, I can say that it was the luncheon reception for Their Royal Highnesses the Duke and Duchess of Cambridge (William and Kate) in June 2011. We knew that the royal couple was most interested in meeting as many young Canadians as possible, so we invited the young chefs from the Junior Culinary Team Canada to assist with the "Celebration of Youth" luncheon as well as students from various culinary school programs from across Canada.

The menu for the luncheon took weeks to develop and it featured products from every province and territory, including arctic delicacies such as Qikiqtarjuaq sea urchin, harvested by an Inuit scuba diver named Charlie, Cape Dorset kelp and Banks Island muskox. The outdoor luncheon was planned to be the main event of the visit. The cooking teams were organized so that one member of the Junior National Culinary Team–usually chefs in their 20s who are at the start of their careers–had his or her team of young sous-chefs, in addition to one Rideau Hall chef. At one point, there were more than 40 aspiring chefs and seasoned professionals in the kitchen! It was a tremendous coordination effort but well worth it. During the press briefing earlier that day, the group of journalists asked to see the kitchen and to take photos of the young chefs at work. I agreed and, as I opened the doors into the kitchen, all I could say was "here they come!" It was organized chaos but a tremendous opportunity for the team members. While the food preparation was going on in the background, I was interviewed by the press corps in the kitchen, where I am truly in my element. Outside of this environment, the interview would have been far more challenging for me!

On the day of the much-anticipated luncheon, which was to take place in the beautiful upper terrace gardens, the weather did not co-operate and the event had to be moved indoors. Nevertheless, we were later told that the luncheon was the highlight of the three-day program and that the royal couple was most appreciative of the efforts put forward by the young chefs as well as by our whole team.

HRH the Duchess of Cambridge thanks Executive Chef Louis Charest and his team following the "Celebration of Youth" luncheon in 2011.
Photo credit: MCpl Dany Veillette, Rideau Hall

Prior to the royal couple's departure from Rideau Hall, staff members who assisted with the visit were assembled to bid farewell to Their Royal Highnesses. Their appreciation for the warm welcome they received was evident and we were grateful for the opportunity. The royal couple left Ottawa to travel to Montréal and, from there, boarded HMCS Montréal, which would take them to Québec for a two-day stay at the Citadelle. Right after the royal couple's departure from Rideau Hall, members of my team and I scrambled to get to Québec to prepare, once again, for their arrival. Seeing familiar faces as they entered the Citadelle must have been reassuring for them since, as soon as Prince William spotted me, he asked if I was following them! Two days later, as the staff prepared for their departure, I stayed behind, not wanting to appear like a royal stalker! As they were leaving, the Prince noticed that I was not there and Their Royal Highnesses came to personally thank me and to say goodbye which, to my surprise, included a hug from the Duchess!

Just a few years earlier, in November 2009, His Royal Highness the Prince of Wales and the Duchess of Cornwall (Prince Charles and Camilla) were in Canada for their first visit since their marriage in 2005. It was an 11-day whirlwind trip across the country, with stops in St. John's, Montreal, Toronto, Vancouver and Victoria and eventually Ottawa. Their program had been quite full, and no official events were planned for the rest of the evening. We were told by the Prince's valet that His Royal Highness and the Duchess were tired and that they would take their dinner in the Royal Suite. To my surprise, the Prince's valet came to the kitchen shortly after the dinner was served and told me that, as soon as Prince Charles saw the food which had been prepared for them, he knew that he was "home" and that they were in good hands for the rest of the visit!

My years at Rideau Hall as the executive chef and as part of a greater team of dedicated employees have been and continue to be both enriching and rewarding. I have cooked for three generations of the royal family – Her Majesty the Queen, His Royal Highness Prince Charles, and His Royal Highness Prince William – and I am hopeful that, during a future visit, I will have the privilege of preparing something special for the youngest Royals! It is truly a pleasure to showcase the best of what Canada's bounty has to offer.

Chef Louis Charest

Executive Chef Louis Charest with TRH the Prince of Wales and the Duchess of Cornwall during a visit to Canada in 2009. Photo credit: MCpl Jean-François Néron, Rideau Hall

CHRISTMAS FOR THE CHILDREN

One of the staff's favorite events at Rideau Hall was the annual children's Christmas party which, many say, dated as far back as Lord and Lady Dufferin who arrived in Ottawa in 1872 with a young family in tow. This party evolved over the years, but it continued to be one of the most anticipated annual events, not only for the young guests but also for the Governors General and their families. During the Christmas party, formalities and protocol were set aside so that children could come to Rideau Hall for what would probably be one of their most exciting childhood memories.

When I first started at Rideau Hall, the Christmas party was organized for children from various community organizations, such as the Ottawa Boys' and Girls' Club and its Francophone counterpart, Le Patro. Most often, the young children were from disadvantaged backgrounds and the anticipation of coming to Rideau Hall was probably almost as exciting as the party. When we saw the kids disembarking from the buses and walking through the front doors, their eyes were as big as marbles and their excitement (and ours) was palpable.

The party was held in the Tent Room which dates back to the beginning of the 19th century. The room was originally used for different purposes, including as an indoor tennis court by day, and a formal room for large dinners by night. Decorative lampposts were moved into the tent-like room along with the dressed tables and silverware and the room was transformed. Since that time, the Tent Room has been renovated, reinforced, and refurbished numerous times but the walls are still covered with a beautiful striped fabric to maintain the tent theme. It was, by far, one of the favorite rooms in the Residence and the perfect room for a children's party! Each year, our staff would decorate a beautiful, majestic tree, usually donated by the Christmas Tree Capital of Canada (a title which was awarded to a different community each year) and we would fill the room with festive garlands and balloons.

Before the start of the party, we would gather all the children in the alcove outside the Tent Room and, at the right moment, the heavy double doors would open to reveal a winter wonderland. The noise level would rise instantly, and all the rules were left behind as the children raced in. At each place setting, they would find noise makers, candy canes and various other treats which we had been shopping for since September!

Once all the children were seated and the noise level had subsided, the aide-de-camp would tell the children that, on the count of three, they needed to make enough noise so that Their Excellencies could hear them and come down to see them. The directions did not have to be repeated a second time – the noise level would increase by several decibels – and Their Excellencies would enter the room to the sound of noisemakers and horns and screams of delight. It would then take a while to settle the children as Their Excellencies greeted them. There were always two children chosen to say Grace and assist the Governor General with carving the turkey. Then, with formalities behind them and with the Governor General's encouragement, the noise level would explode while staff rushed to serve the meal. The turkey and gravy were always popular, but the mashed potatoes were eventually changed to French fries. And even though veggies were added for colour, they were rarely touched! Magicians and games followed, and then Santa arrived, carrying gifts for each child. By the end of the afternoon, they all piled back onto the buses, probably as exhausted as Their Excellencies and the staff but with delightful memories to last a lifetime!

During the LeBlanc mandate, Mr. LeBlanc suggested that the party be moved to other parts of the country so that it could be experienced by children who did not live in Ottawa. We welcomed the idea, and it was agreed that the first children's Christmas party outside of Rideau Hall would be held in Verdun, Quebec, a suburb of Montréal which, at the time, was known for its many pockets of low-income neighborhoods. Mr. LeBlanc asked us to meet with representatives of a group to which Their Excellencies had extended their honorary patronage. When we did the pre-visit, we suggested to the organizers that we could serve hot dogs, hamburgers and fries because the children might prefer this menu over traditional turkey, potatoes, gravy, and vegetables. I immediately saw the look of disappointment on the director's face. He explained to us (the bureaucrats from Ottawa) that these kids would probably never or rarely have a turkey dinner, whereas hot dogs and fries were almost a daily staple for them. We felt terrible. He was right, and we could not have been more wrong. So, turkey it was!

The day before the event, a small group of employees travelled to Verdun to begin preparations for the party. The chosen venue was a church basement which accommodated all our requirements, including a kitchen for the food. We arrived in Verdun with carloads full of decorations, wrapped presents, treat bags and, of course, an outfit for Santa. The staff worked late into the night, transforming the church basement into a magical wonderland with strings of balloons and garlands stretched from one end of the room to the other. Nobody asked for overtime. They were as excited as the children who would see the room for the first time the next day.

Claude Lepage, one of our long-time footmen, always volunteered to be Santa, a role which was clearly more important than the Governor General that day. Once the traditional luncheon and entertainment were over, Santa made his grand entrance to the screams and delight of almost 150 young children. We watched as each child anxiously lined up to speak with Santa, some of them trembling with excitement. At one point, one of the children sitting on Santa's lap gave him such a big hug that it brought tears to Santa's eyes, and to ours. It was another one of those moments when our work was not a job. We knew that, along with the Governor General, we were helping to create "once in a lifetime" memories for these children.

This new tradition of holding the Christmas party in different regions of the country continued for a few years until a number of factors and sensitivities made it increasingly more difficult to host this event. To our great disappointment, the annual children's Christmas party was cancelled in 2002.

Richard Legrand, Maître d'hôtel

Rideau Hall Footman, Claude Lepage, as Santa, with Mrs. Claus, Francine Bellanger, at the annual Children's Christmas Party hosted by the Governor General. Photo credit: Rideau Hall photographer

LORD STANLEY COMES HOME

It was no secret that Governor General Ray Hnatyshyn loved sports and, even more, enjoyed hearing or telling a good story. So, when the 100th anniversary of the Stanley Cup was being planned for 1992, it took very little to convince Mr. Hnatyshyn that the Cup should be returned to Rideau Hall, even for just a visit! The Stanley Cup was named after then Governor General Lord Stanley of Preston, who proclaimed that it would be awarded to Canada's top ice hockey club. Lord Stanley and his entire family enjoyed hockey and it was an ideal way to promote the sport.

As a starting point, we contacted the Hockey Hall of Fame, located in Toronto, to discuss whether they might be interested in holding an event at Rideau Hall, open to the public, where some of the artifacts and memorabilia from the Hall of Fame could be on display, including the much-revered Stanley Cup. Their response was positive and, within weeks, we had confirmed dates for a weekend of special events, including an official opening, a black-tie dinner for some of the legends of the sport and a reception for young hockey players and their volunteer coaches.

The cargo van arrived from Toronto on a Friday morning, carrying numerous trophies, vintage sweaters, photos, hockey sticks and countless other items. The Stanley Cup, however, arrived in its own van, resting comfortably in a large wooden box, and handled only by white-gloved employees of the Hall of Fame. Inside the Tent Room, it sat proudly on its own pedestal!

That evening, Governor General Ray Hnatyshyn hosted a reception and formal dinner, attended by representatives of the National Hockey League, hockey players, referees, sportscasters, and a few famous parents of NHL players! Most of the guests arrived in formal or semi-formal attire, many of them having never visited Rideau Hall before. Of note was hockey legend Bobby Hull, who arrived with a case of beer for the Governor General, a simple token of appreciation for the invitation! The dinner conversations were animated and interesting, and Mr. Hnatyshyn's speech soon became less formal and more entertaining. When came the time for dessert, the coffee was served in the traditional demi tasse cups. I was seated next to the legendary sportscaster, Dick Irvin, who laughed because he could barely hold the tiny gold gilded cup with his hands! He was used to having his coffee in a large paper cup!

The next morning, the public rooms at Rideau Hall were filled with hundreds of young hockey players, along with their coaches and parents, who were invited to visit the exhibit and say hello to some of their hockey heroes. One of the guests recounted how, when he saw the legendary Jean Béliveau standing among a group of young admirers, he approached Mr. Béliveau to thank him for the many years of hockey enjoyment he had provided his fans. Without hesitation, Mr. Béliveau replied that, in fact, it was him, the young volunteer coach, who should be thanked for the early mornings spent teaching and mentoring the kids!

For two full days, the line-up of visitors outside Rideau Hall went all the way down the main drive. It was a wonderful opportunity to fill the large public rooms with youthful enthusiasm and to welcome Lord Stanley's Cup back to its home!

Gabrielle Lappa

THE BIG TIPPER

During earlier mandates, when state visits tended to be longer and full delegations would be accommodated at Rideau Hall for the duration of the visit, it was not unusual for staff members who attended to the delegates or dignitaries throughout the visit to receive gifts or small mementos such as a signed photo, a pen etc. Occasionally, a monetary tip was left, to be divided amongst the staff. It was a different time, and the gifts were appreciated by those who received them. On one occasion, however, we had a visit from an African leader accompanied by a rather large delegation. They stayed at Rideau Hall for a number of days and the employees had worked almost round the clock to support the large delegation. When the president was ready to leave, he called me in to the royal suite and told me that he had never been treated so well in any other place he had visited. He handed me an envelope, a gift of appreciation for our staff, he said. I went to my office, not knowing what was in the envelope but it was heavy. I was completely surprised to see that it was equivalent to several thousand Canadian dollars, from a country not known for being very affluent. Without giving it more than a thought, I did what I had always done in the past, with full approval from our managers. I divided the gift amongst the supervisors for the kitchen, housekeepers, footmen etc., and told them to distribute their portion evenly amongst the staff that had worked on the visit.

Somehow, word of the generous gift got out and I was immediately called into the Secretary's office where I was told that the staff could not keep the money. A call was made to the country's ambassador to say that the money would be returned. However, the ambassador refused to take the money back, saying it would be an insult to the president. It was a delicate situation that caused quite a stir and considerable discontent. In the end, the incident led to the establishment of a gift policy at Rideau Hall which would eventually become standard practice for all government departments.

Richard Legrand, Maître d'hôtel

CHANGING TIMES

When Jeanne Sauvé became Canada's first female Governor General in 1984, we knew that things were going to change. Madame Sauvé was determined to make the necessary modifications to an institution and a building which required some modernization. Although Madame Sauvé was a gracious and lovely lady from the beginning to the end of the mandate, the early years were difficult primarily because of the many changes taking place throughout the Residence. The departure of long-serving individuals who had been part of the organization for many years left a void of tradition and experience which was felt by many. Esmond Butler, who had been the Secretary to six governors general as well as Assistant Press Secretary to Queen Elizabeth for two years, was highly respected amongst the staff. He commanded respect, in part by his stature, but also for his experience and knowledge. And for those of us who worked for him and knew him, he was a true gentleman who brought dignity to the Office.

This was also a time when the relevance of many historic institutions was being questioned, and Rideau Hall was one of them, particularly with respect to cost. We were lagging in terms of technology and much work needed to be done to update the Residence. Significant repairs and a good amount of taxpayer dollars were needed to do the work! Understanding that it would not be easy, Madame Sauvé was determined to see these important changes put into place at Rideau Hall, including incorporating computers for the offices, larger and safer kitchen and pantry areas and, of course, finishing parts of the basement which, in places, still had dirt floors. At the same time, the Tent

Room needed to be renovated and the once beautiful tent-like fabric on its walls had to be replaced, due primarily to the discoloration from many years of smoking in the room.

To make matters worse, there was also a very public battle brewing about access to the grounds of Rideau Hall. The land surrounding the Residence was, and still is, one of the most beautiful park-like settings in Canada. It was a perfect destination for locals and visitors. Unfortunately, little had been done to upgrade security in and around the buildings to provide some protection for those living there, as well as for staff and guests. The black iron gates were always open, and the front and side doors were often left unlocked, perhaps because the assumption was that nobody would wander into Rideau Hall uninvited! There were no security cameras in and around the building and many of us can remember the times when we came across individuals who just walked into the Residence unnoticed. I recall one of them telling me that she was there to see the Queen and another unexpected visitor was found looking at the papers on the Governor General's desk. When I asked his name and how he had entered the Residence, he replied that he had come through the front doors. Easy!

Our footmen often spoke of the many times they were serving lunch or dinner on the terrace or verandah and tourists would wander to the back of the Residence, with no security guard or barrier separating the public from the private areas. Most disturbing was the fact that area residents would often use the long drive leading to Rideau Hall as a shortcut to avoid traffic on Sussex Drive at rush hour. They would enter through the front gate and exit through the back to get to their homes in Rockliffe Park, with no speed limits. And for those of us who lived on the grounds, it was not unusual to see cars coming through the open gates at all hours of the night so that the occupants could conduct their "private business" in the dark, unlit areas. The only risk was that the occasional patrol car might spot them, but even that was unlikely because of the limited number of security guards on site. It was a different time, but for those living in the Residence or on the grounds, it was a concern.

When the matter of closing the grounds was brought to the attention of the Sauvés by the RCMP and representatives of the National Capital Commission, it was to address a number of concerns. The decision to close the front and back gates was a collective one based entirely on the recommendations of the security experts. Throughout it all, there continued to be organized tours of the public rooms, so Rideau Hall was still accessible to Canadians. Unfortunately, the blame for the closing of the grounds was laid entirely on Madame Sauvé and enough noise was made to tarnish the reputation of a great lady. As she had done throughout her career, Jeanne Sauvé did her job with intelligence and grace despite making some decisions that were not popular but nonetheless necessary to bring about improvements and change. For those of us who knew and worked for Jeanne Sauvé, we also knew that she was a kind and considerate individual. As her staff members, we felt her appreciation for all that we did, and we truly felt like we were part of her extended family. It was not unusual for Madame Sauvé to sit and chat with us, almost like a mother speaking to her son or daughter. She always took an interest in her employees and in their families, especially their children. The children's Christmas party was one of her favorite events.

Madame Sauvé was also a very devout woman who had a strong faith. She prayed often and I can recall how honoured and humbled she was when Mother Teresa came to Rideau Hall for a visit. Both women sat together for quite some time and had a long private chat. I was standing close by but not in the room. At one point, Madame Sauvé signaled to me to come in and whispered into my ear that I should go up to her bedroom to get some white socks for Mother Teresa who was wearing sandals on a cold, damp day. When I returned to the room and handed Her Excellency the socks, she gave them to her guest who graciously accepted them and put them in her pocket, saying she would take them for someone who needed them more than her. Two truly great women.

The grounds were eventually reopened after the swearing in of the Rt. Hon. Ramon John Hnatyshyn, but not before a more elaborate security system had been put into place, access cards were given to staff, the entrances protected by security guards and the grounds patrolled at all times. We all felt a bit safer and, undoubtedly, so did the Governors General and their families.

Richard Legrand with Gabrielle Lappa

MOVING RIDEAU HALL–THE G7 SUMMIT

In 1988, the G7 summit was scheduled to take place in Toronto. As is the tradition, Governor General Sauvé was asked to host the world leaders at a state luncheon and the location chosen for this event was the Art Gallery of Ontario. At the time, the Gallery had little that could be used for such an occasion, and the quality of rentals, even in Toronto, left much to be desired back in the 80s. I knew that this was an especially important event, not just for the Governor General but also for Canada. Our country would be hosting world leaders such as President Ronald Regan, British Prime Minister Margaret Thatcher, French President Jacques Mitterrand, and German Chancellor Helmut Schmidt. The event had to be as special as if it were taking place at the official Residence in Ottawa. So, we decided to move Rideau Hall to Toronto. Despite the extra work, the decision to do this greatly increased my comfort level, primarily because I knew, for sure, that we would have what was needed to stage this first-class event. I also knew that the cost of doing it this way would be considerably less than renting everything! Madame Sauvé trusted our decision, so off we went.

For weeks, our executive chef, Michel Pourbaix, worked with a team of chefs from Toronto to plan a menu which would showcase the best of Canadian cuisine for these world leaders. Two days before the event, my crew left Ottawa with an 18-wheeler truck, loaded with everything from the Ballroom chairs to the salt and pepper shakers! I flew to Toronto in advance and was at the door as the truck pulled in.

Assisted by the gallery staff, we unloaded everything, set up the room and prepared for the event in one day. Everything looked beautiful.

As Madame Sauvé entered the room, I can still recall the look of pride on her face, knowing that her guests were about to experience Canada at its best.

State luncheon on the occasion of the G-7 Summit, hosted by the Rt. Hon. Jeanne Sauvé, at the Art Gallery of Ontario in 1988. Among the world leaders were: U.S. President Ronald Regan, British Prime Minister Margaret Thatcher, French President Jacques Mitterrand, and German Chancellor Helmut Schmidt, as well as Prime Minister Brian Mulroney. Background: Maître d'hôtel Richard Legrand. Photo credit: Raynald Kolly, Rideau Hall photographer

AT YOUR SERVICE: FROM
CAPTAIN TO COLONEL

As a member of the Canadian Armed Forces, to be able to work directly for the commander-in-chief is a privilege. Being able to do so in different capacities, at three different times in my career, and for four Governor Generals, was a definite highlight of my 38 years with the Royal 22è Régiment.

I had just flown in from Germany where I was stationed in Lahr. My regiment had put forward my name as a potential candidate for aide-de-camp (ADC) to the Governor General and, even though I knew very little about the position, I was lucky enough to find a Maclean's magazine at the airport with an article about the Office and the incumbent, the Rt. Hon. Edward Schreyer. I took that to be a sign, so I bought the magazine and, before I knew it, I was driving through the gates of Rideau Hall for my interview.

The whole process took the better part of a morning with one-on-one meetings with the principal officers of the Household, ending with the Governor General. A luncheon followed, where I was questioned on domestic and international affairs. At the same time, I knew that, faced with the very elaborate place setting in front of me, my every move was being observed for "suitability!" Two days later, just before returning to Germany, I was informed that I had the job and that I was expected to start in two weeks. Although I was clearly pleased, I knew there were going to be some adjustments to my lifestyle and daily routines!

The Schreyers arrive on Parliament Hill for the opening of Parliament, accompanied by Captain Bernard St-Laurent, Aide-de-Camp in 1979.
Credit: Rideau Hall photographer

From that point on, Rideau Hall was not only the Governor General's official Residence, but it also became my own. At the time, the three serving aides-de-camp had to be single and they had to live at Rideau Hall. The rule had been set out in a manual by A.F. Lascelles, then Secretary to the Earl of Bessborough in 1934, and it had never been updated. "*It has been a rule at Government House that A.D.Cs should be unmarried; apart from the fact that there is no accommodation available for married A.D.Cs, the married state is not really compatible with their duties. A.D.Cs who become engaged are expected to vacate their appointment before marriage.*[7]" So, as in 1934, the three serving aides-de-camp (each respectively from the army, navy and air force) had their quarters on the third floor, right above the

---

7   A.F. Lascelles, Secretary to the Governor General, « *Government House Ottawa* », December 1934, p. 91

main entrance. It was like living above the shop, but with the commander-in-chief and his family down the hall!

Like the aides-de-camp, some members of the Household as well as some support staff in essential positions, such as the valet, the chef and the chauffeurs, also had their living quarters at Rideau Hall or on the grounds. We interacted daily with the vice-regal family and with the staff and we saw each other often. At one point, I even set up a regular TGIF gathering at the end of each week when we weren't travelling or working on events. Our Friday get-togethers became quite popular with "live-in staff" and even Mr. Schreyer showed up on occasion.

The aides-de-camp are visible symbols of the special relationship that exists between Canada's military forces and their commander-in-chief. Their primary duties are to plan and implement the detailed scenarios and logistics of an event, including timings, security requirements, protocol, transportation, accommodations, and other arrangements. In 1980, we did not have the luxury of a computer or the internet so we had to get our information correct the first time, as any change would infuriate the secretaries and delay the printing process on the old Gestetner printer. The daily afternoon tea at 5 p.m., attended by members of the Household and, occasionally, the Governor General was, therefore, the perfect time for the aides-de-camp to get much needed information and to get, from the Household, their commitment to attend and assist with the upcoming events.

With a busy program such as the one taken on by the Schreyers, one aide-de-camp was almost always travelling or on an advance, while the remaining two were on duty. The aide-de-camp in-waiting supports the Governor General while the next-in-waiting supports the spouse and assists with larger events. Although the ADCs are usually quite young in their careers to have such responsibilities, they are, by profession, structured, organized and disciplined so planning events, assigning tasks and keeping an activity on cue was natural for us. We also had the help of an amazing team of hard-working staff members at Rideau Hall, many of whom had at least a decade or two of experience. They were always professional and helped, in many ways, to ensure that everything went as planned. I was still a young officer and, at times, I "dropped a ball or two" but there was always someone on the staff who discreetly rescued me. They were truly the best group of individuals I have had the pleasure of working with.

As mentioned earlier, the aides-de-camp could not be married while serving at Government House. However, this didn't preclude us from enjoying the company of the few young ladies who worked in the Residence. Soon after my arrival at Rideau Hall, I noticed a new secretary, who would regularly come to pick up her morning coffee at the shared coffee pot, which was conveniently located next to my office. I would also see her at lunch in the staff cafeteria. One day, in conversation, I mentioned that my mother was a superb cook, especially when it came to desserts. I added that, if I ever met someone who could make "Nanaimo bars" like my mother, I would marry her. A few days later, this lovely young lady, named Lucie, showed up at my desk with a paper bag containing Nanaimo bars. It was a jaw dropping moment and, soon after, we started to see each other. Unfortunately, my schedule was such that I had very little time off between events. Plus, we wanted to be discreet about our relationship, so we had to rely on "upstairs downstairs" tactics to see each other. Lucie would make her way towards the spiral staircase in the basement which went up to the aides-de-camp's quarters and I would walk through the red-carpet area on the main level, wishing all the members of the Household a good evening as I walked by their offices, on my way to the spiral staircase. Unfortunately, it didn't take long for some staff members to figure out our strategy and I was summoned to the Secretary's office, Mr. Esmond Butler. He told me that he had heard rumours that I was seeing a member of the staff and went on to say that it was not appropriate for an officer of the

Household to be dating a staff member and that it had to stop immediately. Clearly, we had to change our strategies because I was not about to stop seeing this young lady. We figured it out and, once I completed my assignment at Rideau Hall, I kept my word and married Lucie. Almost forty years later, she still makes the best Nanaimo bars!

I returned to Rideau Hall for a second time, but now at the rank of lieutenant-colonel. The position of Director, Program Implementation and Security, was multifaceted. I was responsible for managing the aides-de-camps, the events and the hospitality sections. It also included coordinating with the National Capital Commission for infrastructure maintenance and projects, and with the RCMP for security. The infrastructure portfolio was the most demanding because Rideau Hall is a maintenance nightmare. In 1838, it was a moderately-sized three-story stone villa. Along came Lord and Lady Dufferin who felt that the Residence needed room to entertain more guests. And so, in 1876, the Ballroom and Tent room, (which was used primarily as a tennis court), were added. The front façade, as we know it, was built in 1916. So many changes were made to the Residence over the years that it can be compared to a Lego structure with building blocks that are not necessarily a good fit!

Once or twice a year, we would transfer the Governor General's program to the Citadelle, a national historic site and the home of the Royal 22ᵉ Régiment. I looked forward to being there and I particularly enjoyed my time with the Rt. Hon.Roméo LeBlanc, a former teacher and history buff who kept us on our toes by constantly observing things that we should have noticed before him. During one of our September stays at the Citadelle, Mr. LeBlanc called me into his office and asked me to follow him to the verandah. He pointed to a part of the fortress overlooking the St. Lawrence River, where a large Canadian flag flies high above the water and where the wind is always blowing strong. He asked me if I noticed anything strange. I could not figure out what he was referring to. "Do you see anything unusual there?" he said, pointing to the flag. Sure enough, Mr. LeBlanc was referring to the red panel on the end of the flag which appeared to be considerably narrower than the one on the other side of the maple leaf! Our flag looked seriously unbalanced! It seems that the flag, which is constantly subjected to high winds, frequently ends up tattered and torn on the edge. The Vandoos, my regiment, were known for their ingenious ways of dealing with challenges. In this case, replacing the flag each time the edges frayed was quite costly, so someone decided to extend the life of the flag by clipping the frayed edge and sewing a new seam, eventually shrinking the panel, one inch at a time! Thinking that nobody would notice, they continued to do this until Mr. LeBlanc, the Governor General and their Commander-in-chief, looked out his office window, and noticed. I don't know how long it took but it seemed that, within minutes, a new Canadian flag, with the proper dimensions, was once again flying high above the St-Lawrence!

Terrace overlooking the St-Lawrence at the Citadelle in Québec. The Rt. Hon. Roméo LeBlanc requested that the largest available Canadian flag be flown at the Citadelle.

Planning state visits abroad, in conjunction with the protocol office at Foreign Affairs, was another part of my responsibilities. Among others, I worked on visits to India, Pakistan and Africa for the Rt. Hon. Roméo LeBlanc and to South America for the Rt. Hon. Adrienne Clarkson. The most memorable visit for me was the one to Kosovo. Shortly after her installation, Madame Clarkson met with the Chief of the Defence Staff, General Maurice Baril, and expressed her wish to visit the Canadian troops abroad, in her capacity as commander-in-chief. This was to be a first, as a commander-in-chief had never before travelled to an operational theatre. The complexity was in the secrecy around the travel arrangements, the tactical air and land transportation and the absence of local infrastructure to support this type of visit. In addition to these challenges, it was late fall, and we would be dealing with heavy fog, which limited our air and land movement. Upon arrival, and on our way to our accommodations, a well-trained warrant officer ran ahead of our armoured vehicle for more than 5 kilometers, as our "eyes on the ground." Nothing could be left to chance and, thankfully, all went well. The unexpected visit by the commander-in-chief was deeply appreciated by the troops.

In August 2007, I returned, once again, to Rideau Hall as senior advisor to the Secretary to the Governor General and eventually as deputy secretary of the Policy, Program and Protocol Directorate. The Office, like many others, was undergoing a major reorganization and required someone with experience to focus on priorities and ever-reducing budgets. During that time, I had the privilege of accompanying the Rt. Hon. Michaëlle Jean to the repatriation ceremonies of the deceased military members returning from Afghanistan to Trenton. These events were both moving and emotionally charged, and I watched as Madame Jean, in her role as the commander-in-chief, consoled, supported and reassured the families and friends of the deceased, like few others have been able to do.

As I reflect on my military career, I've been fortunate to have travelled extensively, to have served Governors General in a number of capacities and to have worked with a team of individuals who, through their loyalty, dedication and professionalism, helped to make Rideau Hall a living Residence of which we can all be proud.

Colonel (retired) Bernard St-Laurent, CD

The Rt. Hon. Roméo LeBlanc with Col. St-Laurent at the Citadelle.
Photo credit: Rideau Hall photographer

JUST ANOTHER DAY IN THE
LIFE OF AN AIDE-DE-CAMP

It was Governor General Leblanc's first night at Rideau Hall after a long day of official events, including the installation ceremony in the morning, numerous receptions and a formal dinner in the evening. Prior to becoming the Governor General, it is traditional for the family to stay at Rideau Gate, a Government of Canada guest house just outside the gates of the official Residence, on Sussex Drive. Immediately after the installation ceremony, they arrive at Rideau Hall which will be their home for the next five or more years.

Following a long day of events, the LeBlancs retired to their private quarters on the 2nd floor of the Residence and prepared for bed. I too was starting to unwind after a long but successful program of events. It had been a bitterly cold day and I remember noticing that it was midnight, and I was still wearing my uniform. Within moments of that thought, I heard the fire alarms ringing throughout the Residence! It was an unusual occurrence and, as I ran towards the private apartments, all I could think was that we were not off to a great start with this vice-regal couple! I knocked on the doors of the private quarters. The door opened and there stood the new Governor General and Mrs. Leblanc, in pajamas, looking both startled and half-asleep. I quickly assured them that I would find out what was going on and that I would be back to let them know. Without a word, Mr. LeBlanc looked at me, turned around and went back to bed!

Eighteen months later, at my farewell dinner hosted by the Governor General, Mrs. LeBlanc recalled their first night at Rideau Hall when, in a moment of panic with the fire alarms blaring, she opened the door of their apartment and there, standing at attention, was a young captain in uniform reassuring them that all would be fine. A jarring but comforting introduction to what life would be like at Rideau Hall!

Lieutenant-General Michael John Hood, C.M.M, CD, is a former commander of the Royal Canadian Air Force and a former aide-de-camp to Governors General Ramon J. Hnatyshyn and Roméo LeBlanc.
Photo credit: Bertrand Thibeault

SHATTERED RIBBONS AND BOWS

While working at Rideau Hall, we often witness moments that are a part of a historic event, good or bad. During Canada's centennial year, the Governor General received more than 60 visiting heads of state who, in addition to coming to the nation's capital, also visited the site of Expo 67 in Montréal. One of the more significant visits that year was by President Charles de Gaulle who arrived in Montréal prior to travelling to Ottawa. As part of his speech there, he chose to end it with the famous phrase "Vive le Québec libre!" His words were seen to be a statement of support for Quebec sovereignty, which immediately sparked a diplomatic incident as well as much outrage from then-Prime Minister Lester B. Pearson. As a result, the much-anticipated visit to Ottawa and to Rideau Hall the following day was immediately cancelled by the Prime Minister.

Back at Rideau Hall, the world-renowned Chef Jean Zonda, who himself was French, had been working for weeks on beautiful, large baskets and bows, made entirely of sugar, to be used as centrepieces for the state dinner. Each creation was described as a glistening masterpiece for probably the most significant event in Chef Zonda's career. Within minutes of the Prime Minister's decision to cancel the visit, word was received at Rideau Hall that all preparations for the dinner were to stop. On hearing the news, the Chef was so upset that, in a fit of rage, he went into the pantry, where the sculpted sugar baskets and bows were being stored and smashed them all into pieces. When he left the room, the pantry staff quietly picked up the pieces and took them away so he would not have to see them as a reminder of the visit that never happened.

Gilles (Jimmy) Carrière, Footman

BOLDLY CANADIAN!

As we approached the 90s, a concerted effort was made to showcase all things Canadian at Rideau Hall. Canadian artwork began to have more prominence in the Residence despite the British aristocrats who looked down on us from their gold gilded frames in the main hallway and public rooms.

In the kitchen and pantry, our chefs and staff became experts in Canadian food specialties including culinary delights such as caribou, unique cheeses and even chocolates made by Trappist monks in a monastery in Quebec! And, naturally, Canadian wines replaced the French wines at our events. We knew that Rideau Hall was considered the "trend setter" for how things should be done at the highest level of Canadian hospitality.

I will never forget the event when we were hosting our newly minted Canadian heads of mission, and a relatively new wine, a Baco Noir, was served to our unsuspecting guests. It was a bold, heavy, fruity wine which was pleasant enough to drink. Unfortunately, it soon became apparent that the choice of wine was unwise. All of us working the event were horrified when we began to notice very visible purple staining on our guests' lips, teeth and dentures, the obvious evidence of a young wine.

Not a word was mentioned during the reception but, rest assured, there was a very interesting "post-event discussion" the next day. And, quite apart from the unexpected "colour" that was added to the soirée, our head housekeeper angrily informed us that it was impossible to remove the stains from the tablecloths! Lesson learned!

JoAnn MacKenzie, Director of Finance

PRESIDENTIAL DESSERT

President Nixon visited Rideau Hall in 1972 and, for the occasion, I had prepared a special dessert for the state dinner. It was called "café liégeois," a coffee infused ice cream served in a chocolate mold. As the President was leaving the Residence, the staff was lined up in the Front Foyer to bid him farewell. Mr. Nixon spotted me in the crowd and told me that, if I had any of that extraordinary dessert left over, I should send it to his plane so he could "take some home to the White House!" Needless to say, I was both honoured and flattered.

Pastry Chef Adrien Joanis (Michener, Léger mandates)

THE STEEL LADIES

We were nicknamed "the steel ladies" because we worked in a small room off the kitchen where the countertops, tables and carts were all made of stainless steel. Everything glistened. Our work included making tea and coffee and preparing for the high tea at the end of the afternoon.

I began working at Rideau Hall in 1967, as Governor General Michener and Mrs. Michener were just moving in. One morning, I was summoned to the dining room by Mr. Michener. He said "Good morning Mrs. Buckland. How many tea bags do you put in the teapot?" I replied, "Three Sir." "Well, from now on, only use two. Just think of the savings at the end of the year and, as a matter of fact, if I'm not in the dining room, don't make tea. Let them drink coffee." As I walked away, a keen-eared footman standing outside the dining room said, "Fancy the Governor telling an English lady how to make tea!"

The next morning, I was very busy in the steel room when a footman dashed in and whisked away His Excellency's hot silver tea pot, without the tea bags, as I had only poured hot water in the pot to warm it up. After Mr. Michener's first sip of nothing but hot water, I half expected the order to come down to go back to three bags!

I especially loved all the pomp and ceremony of royal visits. Queen Elizabeth II liked lemon tarts with her afternoon tea. She surprised me one day by ordering a peanut butter sandwich! Another one of her favorites, which I enjoyed making, were shaved cucumber sandwiches!

I thoroughly enjoyed my years of service at Rideau Hall. There were so many good times like the state and royal visits, the picnics, the garden parties and especially the camaraderie we enjoyed with the staff. [8]

Louisa J. Buckland (Michener and Léger mandates)

---

8   Louisa J. Buckland, Quote from Employee Reunion Collection, 1992

A LOST TREASURE – THE
CITADELLE FIRE OF 1976

The Governor General's Residence at the Citadelle in Québec brings many warm and some sad memories to mind. This Residence is considerably smaller in size than Rideau Hall, making it more intimate, but just as majestic because of its location high atop the cliffs overlooking the St. Lawrence River. The Residence itself is one of several historic buildings set inside the Citadelle, the oldest military fortress in Canada. The Citadelle is also the home of the Royal 22ᵉ Régiment, more commonly known as the Vandoos who, in their red scarlet uniforms and bearskin hats, post sentries at the entrance to the vice-regal Residence when the Governor General is present.

For as long as I can recall, Governors General and their families have loved spending parts of their summers and sometimes the autumn months at the Citadelle. Like Rideau Hall, the Residence reflects our past and the walls of each room are literally and figuratively thick with history. The smaller and more intimate quarters and the spectacular views overlooking the St. Lawrence seemed to re-energize the vice-regal couples and anyone travelling with them.

Each year, when the time came for the Citadelle program to begin, there was almost a sense of excitement amongst our staff, like a family preparing to move to the cottage at the end of the school year. Sheets were draped over the furniture at Rideau Hall; the truck was loaded with supplies and a few of us travelled ahead to clean, dust and stock the kitchen and pantry, trying to anticipate every need. Once there, we always shopped locally, paying cash for our purchases, and making sure to spread the business around to all the merchants in the area. Our suppliers were happy to see us and took great pride in supplying their specialties for the Governor General. Everyone knew we were in town!

Except for a brief vacation period, the Governor General's program continued as it would at Rideau Hall, receiving dignitaries and new ambassadors to Canada, hosting ceremonies and events and visiting communities in the area. For the staff, the Citadelle felt like a home, with most of our rooms being in the basement, under the kitchen area. Our days were long, starting with early breakfast service and often ending after dinner and after every guest had left the Residence. Despite the late hours, we would often walk down the hill, following the massive stone walls of the fort, to enjoy an hour or two of the vibrant city. Occasionally, we were invited to the military mess hall after hours for a beer at the bargain price of 5 cents a can! There was always something to do!

When word of the fire at the Citadelle broke on February 2nd, 1976, our hearts froze. The news was on all the TV and radio stations, and they reported that most of the rooms in the Governor General's Residence had been destroyed or severely damaged. Many of us cried just thinking of what was lost that day.

After a few weeks, we were asked to go to the Citadelle to see the extent of the damage and to see if anything could be salvaged. When we arrived in front of what was once a beautiful building, I stood and cried. The huge iron beams had melted. Our rooms were in a big hole and everything was black. It looked like a disaster zone. The Dining Room, which had always been used for family meals, was not completely destroyed because of a firewall, but there was so much water frozen around the furniture that we found ourselves walking on the long wooden dining table. The satin covered chairs, used for that famous photo taken in 1943 during the Quebec Conference with

Winston Churchill, Mackenzie King and Franklin D. Roosevelt on the terrace of the Citadelle were stuck in ice, as were the silver platters, candelabras and cutlery. Almost everything had to be replaced.

The Rt. Hon. Jeanne Sauvé in the Dining Room at the Citadelle with Maître d'hôtel Richard Legrand. The Dining Room was not destroyed in the fire because of a firewall but it was seriously damaged by smoke and water.
Photo credit: Rideau Hall photographer

It took several years to rebuild the section that was destroyed. Piece by piece, we replaced the crystal and linens. New china was ordered from Spode. Unfortunately, many items were lost, damaged or disappeared.

The actual re-design of the Residence was a huge project. Some of the new rooms were different from the original ones and were met with mixed reviews, primarily because of the modern elements that were incorporated. The official opening of the newly rebuilt Residence took place in 1984 at the start of the Sauvé mandate, eight long years after the fire.

Richard Legrand, Maître d'hôtel

SHORTBREAD AND CHANDELIERS

My first memory of Rideau Hall was in 1979, when I was twelve years old. A family friend invited us to attend the Governor General's Levee, a traditional event which was held on New Year's Day and which was open to the public in the afternoon, after the formal visits by diplomats and politicians in the morning. Visitors would line up outside the Residence, sometimes in very cold weather, to make their way through the public rooms to eventually shake hands with the vice-regal couple, Ed and Lilly Schreyer at the time. For those of us who had never been in the Residence, it was like entering a palace with all its formalities. The rooms were large, and the walls were covered with artwork, including Queen Victoria's portrait in the Ballroom, overseeing the events of the day. The Ballroom was illuminated by a chandelier the size of a small car with what seemed to be thousands and thousands of crystal pendants. I learned, many years later, that the one-ton Waterford crystal chandelier includes 12,000 pieces of crystal and 80 light bulbs. It was a gift from the British government to thank Canada for its contribution to the war effort. It is lowered twice a year and polished one crystal at a time! Christmas poinsettias were everywhere and a majestic Christmas tree, taller than any I had ever seen, lit up the Tent Room. The best part, of course, were the refreshments which were served to everyone after they had gone through the receiving line. Tables were filled with cookies and Christmas treats, and the footmen, dressed in dark suits and ties, walked around with silver trays, serving guests. I can still taste the delicious shortbread cookies I ate that day, served to me by a young footman named Jimmy who was 17 when he started to work at Rideau

Hall. Little did I know at that time that we would someday become colleagues and friends for many years.

My first day working for the Governor General's Office was in 1989. I was just 22 years old and, like many new employees starting at Rideau Hall, this was a world which was completely unknown to me. To add to my level of anxiety, my assignment was to work for the Canadian Heraldic Authority, something that was even further removed from my world! Mr. Robert Watt, the Chief Herald and one of the world's top experts in the field of heraldry, was going to be my boss and all I could think was that my learning curve was going to be pretty steep and that my time at Rideau Hall would be short-lived! Funny how things work out. Surrounded by a team of knowledgeable and dedicated employees led by Mr. Watt, I quickly learned that the Canadian Heraldic Authority is part of the Canadian Honours System and that the Governor General is responsible for the granting of new coats of arms, flags and badges to individuals, groups and organizations. The small team at the Authority included experts in the fields of history and heraldry as well as artists and production staff, all of whom were passionate about telling a story through the use of symbols, colour and words. I truly admired their dedication and I learned from them.

One of the highlights of my time at Rideau Hall came when, shortly after starting to work there, I attended the employee Christmas party and was invited by the aide-de-camp to sit at Governor General Jeanne Sauvé's table. The aide told me that Madame Sauvé enjoyed meeting new employees and spending time with her staff. I quickly agreed and was escorted to the seat right next to Her Excellency! I knew that when Jeanne Sauvé was appointed as Canada's first female Governor General, she had not been well, and the installation ceremony had to be delayed. However, on the day of the ceremony, I remember Madame Sauvé arriving at the Senate Chambers dressed in a beautiful grey silk taffeta gown looking gracious and elegant. Years later, the youngest employee on a staff of 125 was being invited to sit with this great lady! Of course, panic set in for a moment, not knowing which fork to use, when to speak and what to say! So, I watched and copied Her Excellency's moves, and it did not take long before I was able to relax and enjoy the party. Madame Sauvé was a delight to work for.

Following my time with the Canadian Heraldic authority, I worked in Human Resources at Rideau Hall for almost 18 years. Many would agree that working in this field is never easy, but it can be far more complicated when a government department is also a Residence and home to the Governor General and his or her family as well as a workplace to employees whose job descriptions are unlike others in the public service. I received much of my training from my mentor, Danielle Brissette, who navigated the intricacies of the office with expertise and a commitment to making things work.

Years later, I moved into different positions within the Residence, ending as the executive assistant to the Secretary. I had learned so much about the daily workings of the Residence and felt comfortable and confident working with a team of colleagues who were knowledgeable and dedicated. Many of us had worked together for a good number of years and we were like family. We had shared weddings, births, and sad times together and we were always there for each other. The end of one mandate and the start of a new one always came with some trepidation, but we knew that, even though there would be a few newcomers with the newly appointed Governor General, our team would be there to help ease them into life in the big house.

*Chantal Charbonneau at work in her makeshift office during a state visit
to Stockholm with Governor General David Johnston.
Photo credit: Rideau Hall photographer*

Working for Governor General David Johnston and his Secretary, Stephen Wallace, was among the highlights of my career. I was invited to accompany the official delegation on a state visit to Sweden in 2017. The travelling team included long-time colleagues who worked in the planning and hospitality sections as well as office support, logistics coordinators and protocol officers from the department of Global Affairs Canada. The official delegation included VIPs, parliamentarians, and businesspeople in addition to several accomplished Canadians from different walks of life who were there to forge and strengthen relationships with counterparts in the country we were visiting. Among the most popular delegates was hockey great Daniel Alfredsson representing Canada in his native country. Their Excellencies were received at the Royal Palace by King Carl XVI Gustaf and Queen Silvia of Sweden, with all the pomp and circumstance imaginable. Behind the scenes of these formal events, however, could be quite different, simply because of the pace of the events and the long days. Fortunately for us, Mr. Johnston was quite independent but the delegates, many of whom were not used to such a schedule, required some "herding" and hand holding! And although we were used to working long days at Rideau Hall, nothing compared to working on a state visit. That said, the events went off as planned and, even if they did not, our team made it all look seamless! Our days would start early in the morning and rarely end before 1:00 a.m. We were often too tired to think about it but, during those long evenings in our makeshift offices, even a simple gesture, a mis-pronounced word or a spilled glass of water would send us all into a fit of uncontrollable laughter and the occasional tear from exhaustion. The comradery and dedication of our staff made it all easier.

What a privilege to have been at Rideau Hall for most of my working years, to have met many great Canadians and, more impor-tantly to have learned from so many dedicated and experienced indi-viduals, including Jimmy, the footman who served me that delicious shortbread when, as a twelve-year-old, I first set foot in Rideau Hall.

Chantal Charbonneau

Rideau Hall shortbread cookies. Photo credit: Rideau Hall photographer

Rideau Hall Shortbread Cookies

4 1/8 cups all purpose flour

1 ¼ cups icing sugar

1 lb unsalted butter, at room temperature

1 tsp. salt

1 tsp. vanilla extract

Sift flour and icing sugar and set aside.

Cream butter with icing sugar and salt. Mix just until combined. Stir in sifted flour and mix until fully incorporated.

Divide the dough into two equal portions. Roll each portion into a 30cm log. Wrap each log in plastic wrap and chill for at least one hour or for several days.

Preheat oven to 350 degrees.

Set the logs onto a clean cutting board and slice into evenly sized rounds. Placed chilled rounds onto a parchment-lined baking tray, evenly spaced.

Bake for 6-12 minutes (depending on the oven) or until the edges are a pale, light golden brown. Be cautious with the first batch to avoid overbaking. Once you have successfully baked a tray, note the length of cooking time for the next batch. Bake one tray at a time for even baking.

Cool cookies on a wire rack. Enjoy immediately or store in an airtight container for up to 10 days. Yields approx. 50 to 60 cookies.

Possible additions to the shortbread: chopped candy cane bits, chopped nuts, chunks of milk, dark or white chocolate.

Recipe provided by executive chef Louis Charest.

BROOMBALLS AND BOWTIES

Mr. Michener was known for his punctuality. If dinner was scheduled for 8:00 p.m., he expected it to be at 8:00 p.m. and not 8:01! The only time we weren't on a strict schedule was when we played broomball. The pantry staff had a broomball team and, once a week, we played against other teams from the Department of Public Works or the National Capital Commission. The games were on the ice rink at Rideau Hall and, on those evenings, Mr. Michener liked to come down to drop the ball and watch the game. We all enjoyed having His Excellency there to cheer us on but, of course, for most of us, that meant that we had to scramble after the game to change from our sporting gear back into our dark suit and white gloves. As always, dinner was served on time even though a few of us were still hurting from the game!

Gilles (Jimmy) Carrière

Caption: The Micheners with the Rideau Hall broomball team in 1967. Back row, 3rd and 4th from left are then-footmen Jimmy (Gilles) Carrière and Richard Legrand. Photo credit: Rideau Hall Archives

THE ICE STORM OF JANUARY 1998

I will never forget the first day of the famous ice storm that hit most of Eastern Ontario and Western Quebec, not only because of the impact and devastation in the region but also because it coincided with the day I was diagnosed with a chronic inflammatory joint disease developing in my spine. My doctor informed me that day that this was a serious and debilitating illness, and that stress was not helping it. Concerned by the prognosis, and despite the worsening weather conditions, I made my way back to Rideau Hall. I had never taken more than a day or two of sick leave throughout my many years of service and now I needed to tell the Secretary, Madame Judith LaRocque, that I was going to be away from work for at least six months. It was very difficult for me and it became even more so when Madame LaRocque's reaction to the news was astonishment, concern and then panic. "What will we do without you?" she said. I never expected to be in this position despite some of the signs that I ignored.

That same day, when Governor General LeBlanc was told the news, he asked to see me in his office. He said to me, "Richard, your health is more important than Rideau Hall. We will miss you but go home and take care of yourself." The LeBlancs cared very much about their employees who were like family for them. Hearing Mr. LeBlanc's words that day helped me to accept the diagnosis.

At the time of the ice storm, I lived in a house located on the grounds, with my aging mother. The massive power outage had affected the whole area, including Rideau Hall and all the buildings on the grounds. Thankfully, Rideau Hall did have a generator, which I had insisted that Public Works install months earlier when we almost had to cancel a state dinner because of a power failure. When the ice storm hit the region, the LeBlancs invited everyone living on the grounds to come into Rideau Hall to stay warm. As a precaution, we prepared wood to use in the fireplaces just in case the generator stopped working. Rideau Hall may be a grand old house, but it is also a drafty old building, so we had to be prepared. Unfortunately, most of the fireplaces had not been used in years, so we also had to be particularly cautious, especially since a new sprinkler system had been installed throughout the Residence just a short time earlier. We didn't want to be the reason for setting it off!

The next day, and for weeks after, since our kitchen was still functional and some of the staff had been able to make their way in to work, we decided to help out the communities in the immediate and surrounding areas that were completely in the dark. The chefs, pantry and office staff pitched in to cook and deliver casseroles like shepherd's pies and lasagnas to local community centres and schools being used as shelters. Madame LeBlanc went along with the drivers and staff members to deliver the food and to bring teddy bears to the small children. Funds were raised among the staff to help purchase a generator for an employee's family living on a farm who could not leave their animals unattended. There was a daily "check-in" system set up to ensure that colleagues who could not come to work were doing okay. It was a difficult time for everyone affected in far reaching communities in Eastern Ontario and Western Quebec, but it was also heartwarming to see the Rideau Hall family rallying together to help their fellow employees as well as those forced to live in shelters until power could be restored.

Richard Legrand, R.V.M. Footman and Maître d'hôtel at Rideau Hall

PEOPLE, PLANS
AND PROTOCOL

"Like at Buckingham Place, there was a pecking order amongst staff that had to be respected. The senior footman gave the orders, and the junior footmen took the orders. In the dining room, the senior footman stood at the front of the room while the junior was the runner. Everyone had their place!"

Richard Legrand, footman & maître d'hôtel

PROTOCOL

"As Canada evolved, so did Rideau Hall. Changes were wrought by the people who lived and worked here; all were committed to enhancing it. "

Gerda Hnatyshyn, C.C.

The Office of the Governor General has no parallel, and Rideau Hall or the Citadelle is the showcase of the nation where the Governor General receives heads of state and other dignitaries on behalf of Canada, and where we choose to honour our country's most deserving citizens. If our Governors General are to perform their role efficiently, those persons involved in vice-regal events should be well informed about the Residence and its history. Every event should be given a special significance for those who are being received or honoured, as this may be their only encounter with the Governor General. It means planning ahead, reducing risks and providing a clear operational framework that everyone understands, from the footmen to the aides to the Governor General. All one needs to recall is that protocol is not there to intimidate but rather to facilitate. It is there to make people feel comfortable and to ensure all goes smoothly. In all of this, the one basic rule that should be remembered is that effective protocol is made up of good sense, a caring approach for one's guests and the desire to do things with dignity and style.

Ted J. Arcand, Rideau Hall, 1994, Senior Advisor, Protocol, Rideau Hall

---

9   Gerda Hnatyshyn, *Rideau Hall: Canada's Living Heritage*, Ottawa, 1994, p.3

PEOPLE, PLANS AND PROTOCOL

My father served in World War II, with the Régiment de la Chaudière and the Royal 22ᵉ Régiment. We lived in Victoriaville and, as a young teenager, I can recall my parents getting ready to leave for Québec, all dressed up, to attend a formal event hosted by General Georges Vanier, a founding member of the Regiment. My father often spoke of this great man and, even as a young person, I had much admiration and respect for him. The invitation card read *"Cravate noire, robe longue et décorations"* (Black tie, long dress, with decorations). It was my first introduction to the formal world of protocol. A few years later, a one-day class trip to Ottawa brought me to the front gates of Rideau Hall. Being there left a vivid impression on me, and I knew, instinctively, that I wanted to get a better glimpse of the world beyond those gates.

When I first started at Rideau Hall, the responsibility for sending invitations and preparing table plans was held primarily by the aides-de-camp, something which, I suspect, was not part of their basic training. The three young officers, each representing one branch of the armed forces, were recommended to Rideau Hall via their career managers and submitted to a vigorous interview process which included members of the Household and ultimately the Governor General. The selected candidates were often at the top of their class and chosen for their personalities but also for their attention to detail and their ability to react quickly to solve a problem or avert an incident.

My newly created position working with the aides-de-camp came with a number of challenges, which almost made me yearn for my former job at Foreign Affairs. Working in protocol often involves long days and rapidly changing priorities, especially when dealing with the diplomatic corps. So, when Claude Sirois, who was the attaché at Rideau Hall, contacted me to say that there might be a similar position at Government House dealing with protocol and guest lists for the Governor General, it definitely sparked some interest. Before I knew it, I received an invitation from the aide-de-camp, on behalf of Governor General and Madame Léger, to come to Rideau Hall! A few days later, my interview consisted of a luncheon with Their Excellencies and a few members of the Household. The Légers took great interest in their staff and surrounded themselves with people with whom they were comfortable. Their staff was like their family. Nervous as I was when I entered the Residence that day, my mind went back to the moment when our school bus from Victoriaville, Quebec, pulled up to the front of 1 Sussex Drive. I remember peering through the gates, imagining the magnificent Residence and the people who lived there.

There was so much to take in during the interview lunch which was served in the small dining room. I remember my concern about making a *faux pas* and then making the conscious decision to just 'watch and follow'. Much as I tried to eat, every time I was about to put something in my mouth, someone asked a question. Towards the end of the luncheon, Mme Léger stood up and, speaking on behalf of her husband, looked directly at me said "On se revoit bientôt." ("We will see you again soon.") And, just like that, the interview was over. A few weeks later, I arrived at Rideau Hall and stayed for 32 years.

It took a while for the Aides to trust me enough with the responsibilities of the new position and to know that they could count on me. Two years after I started in the new position, we worked on the royal visit to mark the Queen's silver jubilee. It was a lengthy visit but, thankfully, the events were successful and went off without a glitch. As soon as the royal visitors departed, we collapsed, happy but tired!

The aide-de-camp in-waiting for the visit was a young naval officer named Lt(N) Bob Smith. After the departure, Mr. Esmond Butler, the Secretary to the Governor General, came into the aides' office, which was next to ours, and thanked Lt(N) Smith and the other aides for their hard work. It was then that Lt(N) Smith said to Mr. Butler that he could not have done it without my help and the help of my colleague, Rosemary Hales. Realizing that the planning team had grown, Mr. Butler turned and thanked us. He was sincere in his appreciation and it was at that moment that I felt I truly belonged at Rideau Hall.

Esmond Butler was a giant of a man, tall, elegant, and always in control. Before an event, he would come into our office with his glasses on the end of his nose and, with a few simple words, would demonstrate his confidence in us. He always asked "Madame Bellanger, will we be ready?" to which I would always reply "Of course we will Mr. Butler!" He knew the answer to his question before he asked it! He would then turn and go back to his office or rush home to change into his formal attire for the evening.

The working relationship between Mr. Butler and most of his staff was interesting. He commanded respect and, although there were elements of an upstairs/downstairs relationship, he trusted us, and we did our best not to let him down. It was not unusual to see Mr. Butler, seated alongside the staff at a large table covered with piles of invitation cards and envelopes, lending a hand to the frantic 'writing bee' for invitations to the Garden Party or the annual Levee. In fact, he often convinced other Household members to do the same. Back then, we would send more than 10,000 handwritten invitation cards to Canadian dignitaries, parliamentarians, the diplomatic corps, and to anyone who had signed the guest book at the front of the Residence. Fortunately, this tradition was eventually replaced with a simple invitation to the public, published in both languages in local newspapers. What a relief!

One of the most challenging tasks in our work was the preparation of table plans for major events. In addition to ensuring that the list of precedence was respected when preparing the plans, we also had to be aware, as much as possible, of religious, political, and geographic sensitivities as well as personal likes and dislikes. We always tried to seat people with others who might have similar interests or who might benefit from the new contacts. Once the guest list was approved by the Secretary and Their Excellencies, then came the onerous task of seating the guests in the right place. We worked with a large 3 x 4ft plank of wood to replicate a floor plan of the ballroom, with miniature wooden rectangles or circles for the tables, which would then be placed on the sheet of wood, just as the tables would be placed in the ballroom. Each of the guests' names were calligraphed by hand on tiny cards, the size of half a business card, and then placed around the 'mock tables' so that each seating plan could be visualized and changed if necessary. It was not unusual to see this large plank of wood on the floor with two or three staff members kneeling around it, including, occasionally, Mr. Butler. Place cards would sometimes be moved just before a big dinner. A last-minute cancellation, a public political spat earlier that day or mounting diplomatic tensions could wreak havoc on the best laid plans! The seating order would then be typed or sometimes scribbled onto a piece of paper and one of us would run down to the Ballroom to place the name cards on the tables, sometimes as guests were arriving!

One of the most challenging events of my time at Rideau Hall, but perhaps also the most rewarding, was planning for the reception hosted by Governor General Jeanne Sauvé for His Holiness Pope John Paul II in 1984. We knew the challenges that lay ahead, with the first being space and the second being security. In calculating the names of Canadians on the list of precedence, the church leaders, the diplomatic corps and representatives from various organizations, the head count was going to surpass 1500! I panicked when I reached 1700!

During the days leading up to the visit, we received countless telephone calls asking for an invitation to the event, to which we could honestly say that the guest list was closed and that no other names could be added. There were many disappointed people. Among the many calls I received, one, in particular, stood out for me. It was from an elderly gentleman with a soft and humble voice. He told me that his name was Major-General Stefan Sznuk and he asked if it might be possible to be invited to the reception so that he could speak to the Pope. He explained that he had met the Pope when they were both in Krakow during the war. Wojtyla (the Pope) was the Bishop at the time and Mr. Sznuk was the Chief of Police. Attending the reception clearly meant so much to him. Although I explained that the guest list was closed and that no other names could be added, Mr. Sznuk again asked if I could please intercede on his behalf and ask Madame Sauvé if she might consider making an exception. Something about the gentleman intrigued me. I learned that he was 88 years old and that he was the last Polish army and air force attaché in Canada before the Soviets took control of his country. After the demobilization of the Polish army, he settled in Canada. In 1970, Mr. Sznuk was appointed to the Order of Canada for helping over 4,500 Polish veterans emigrate here after World War II. His story touched me and, even though I knew what the answer would be, I promised to check if just one more name could be added to the list.

The next day, during a meeting with Their Excellencies to discuss the upcoming event, I presented Mr. Sznuk's request and, as expected, the answer was, regretfully, no. We were already way beyond the legal capacity for the rooms. I understood but, two days later, I thought that I might try one more time. And then another. Madame Sauvé was a kind woman with a strong faith. She understood my persistence and eventually agreed to include Mr. Sznuk's name on the guest list. Mr. Sauvé, on the other hand, joked with me about being relentlessly stubborn! Each time he saw me, he would jokingly call me "Madame Bellanger, la têtue!" (which meant that I was hard- headed!) I was delighted with Madame Sauvé's decision and conveyed the invitation to Major-General Sznuk!

Planning for the event was a logistical challenge. Movement through the rooms and the crowds of people was not going to be easy. We hoped and prayed for the best! On the day of the event, as the more than 1700 guests started to arrive, staff members would escort guests to their designated rooms throughout the Residence. A large tent had also been set up on the upper terrace where parliamentarians would be gathered. The plan was for His Holiness to move throughout the rooms and the tent in the garden to ensure that all the guests had an opportunity to see the Pope.

When His Holiness arrived, he moved through each room with ease, accompanied by the Sauvés and the Prime Minister and Mrs. Mulroney. He then moved into the large tent where a few hundred parliamentarians had gathered and eventually back into the Residence through the verandah, a small but beautiful room with comfortable seating.

Purely by coincidence, or fate, I was assigned to the Long Gallery, a large gallery-style room, adjacent to the verandah. As I cast an eye over the room, which was quickly filling up, I saw an elderly gentleman who appeared to be a bit frail. He kept glancing at something he held in his hands. I approached him and asked if he might be Major-General Sznuk. His face immediately lit up and, with a warm smile, he said, "Madame Bellanger!". He showed me the medals he had received, which he wanted to show to the Pope. I took him by the hand and led him to the verandah where he could be comfortably seated while waiting for His Holiness and where he might be able to exchange a few words in a less noisy environment. It was the perfect spot for him.

As His Holiness made his way through the larger rooms and the tent, eventually moving towards the verandah, the anticipation could be felt among the guests. When the Pope entered the room, he looked as calm and serene as if he were just arriving for a visit despite having shaken the hands of well over 1,500 guests by that time. Mr. Sznuk was sitting but stood as soon as he spotted His Holiness. Madame Sauvé had noticed the elderly gentleman and, having been briefed on his story, immediately brought Pope John Paul over to see him. The expressions on their faces left little doubt of the warmth and emotions they were feeling. They spoke for a short while in Polish and then, to my surprise, Madame Sauvé took my arm and introduced me to His Holiness, explaining that I had been a key person, not only in the planning of the event but also in the reunion with Major-General Sznuk. The Pope took my hand and held it with a firm gentleness, his piercing blue eyes looking directly at me and his smile warming my heart. It was a moment I will never forget.

After three weeks of working around the clock to ensure the success of the reception, we were able to stand back and see the results. Each of us was proud of the small contribution we had made to the event as was Madame Sauvé. Our respect and appreciation were mutual.

After almost 15 years working with the events team, my career path led me to the information office at Rideau Hall where I was able to combine my previous experience and my interest in the arts and graphics to plan and design exhibits showcasing Canadian artists, historical events, the highlights of each Governor General's mandate, educational materials for schools, promotional material for the Residences as well as the annual Christmas card. Regardless of the jobs we did or the Governors General we served, our work was unique and rewarding.

And the loyalty within the teams of dedicated employees allowed us to look beyond the challenges and to be profoundly grateful for the opportunities.

Francine Bellanger, Planning and Protocol & Information Office

The Rt. Hon. Jeanne Sauvé introducing Francine Bellanger to His Holiness Pope John Paul II at the reception for more than 1700 guests at Rideau Hall. Photo credit: Rideau Hall photographer

UP, UP AND AWAY

When the Governor General's Residence at the Citadelle was rebuilt following the catastrophic fire of 1976, a special event was planned to mark the re-opening. Rebuilding the Residence had taken almost eight years and Madame Sauvé recognized the importance of the landmark, both to the military and civilian communities in Quebec.

Planning for the event became an enormous task with over 500 guests invited to a formal dinner. Since the ballroom could not accommodate nearly that many people, it was decided that this would be an outdoor event, under a beautiful tent placed in the open area immediately in front of the Residence. The staff was a bit apprehensive about this decision, particularly since we had witnessed, on a number of occasions, the effect of the powerful winds from the St. Lawrence River on items and structures which appeared to be firmly secured, including a good number of Canadian and vice-regal flags floating down the mighty river. Nevertheless, planning for the event continued in the hopes that the winds would be in our favour that evening.

While we were setting up, the skies were as clear and as blue as can be, and everything went well. We had purchased beautiful lanterns which hung from the ceiling of the tent and huge colourful vases of flowers adorned the space. The main tables for the buffet dinner as well as 50 tables of 10 to accommodate everyone had been set up. Even the cannons at the front of the Residence were part of the décor.

Following the cocktails which were served in the newly refurbished rooms to allow guests to visit the Residence, everyone was directed through the front doors and into the tent for dinner. As the first few guests were being shown to their tables, a huge gust of wind came off the St. Lawrence. The entire tent lifted 3 feet off the ground, cement posts and all - almost like a balloon. We even felt it in our ears! We all stared in disbelief but, before panic could set in, and as quickly as the tent had lifted, it came back down on the exact spot where it had been just moments before. Not a thing was broken, and the event went on, as planned.

That evening, we were all convinced that we had witnessed a small miracle!

Richard Legrand, Maître d'hôtel

THE ACADIAN STAR

Roméo LeBlanc was the 8th Canadian Governor General, and the first Acadian appointed to the Office. Mr. LeBlanc was also a great storyteller and frequently shared with us the culture and traditions of Acadians in Canada. He liked to test our limited knowledge of Acadian culinary specialties such as "*la poutine râpée*", a traditional Acadian dish that consists of a boiled potato dumpling with a pork filling, or "*les tétines de souris*", a local delicacy also known as sea asparagus! Of course, we laughed at the names of these specialties and, in turn, he laughed at us when we tried to guess what they were. Before long, everyone in the kitchen and pantry had learned and tasted these specialties and they became regular items on our menus, much to the delight of our guests.

One of the highlights of Mr. LeBlanc's mandate was hosting the closing luncheon for the 8th Summit of La Francophonie, a large gathering of more than 50 heads of state from Francophone countries around the world. The Summit was being held in Moncton, New Brunswick and the proposed site for the closing luncheon was Memramcook, a small town of less than 5,000 people outside of Moncton, where Mr. LeBlanc had grown up and attended the Collège Saint-Joseph, the first francophone university in Eastern Canada. Established in 1864, the college was housed in a stately old building nestled in the picturesque Memramcook Valley surrounded by rolling hills. Over the years, the college had been converted into a school for hospitality. Not only did the location have a special meaning for Mr. LeBlanc but it was also special for the students there. Being able to witness and work together with the team from Rideau Hall on an event of this magnitude was an experience they would never forget.

Before a final decision was made on the location, Mr. LeBlanc asked me to visit the former college to assess the site, knowing full well that his expectations might have been unrealistic. I must admit that I, too, did not expect much, knowing only that we would be dealing with a very small community and a very old building! The drive there was pleasant and picturesque, and I soon came upon the college, sitting high on a hill, surrounded by acres of greenery (and a wonderful golf course!). Before long, I realized that, with a few small miracles, this wonderful old building could be perfect for our event. As excited as I was to visit the school, the staff and students who were there to learn about the fine art of hospitality were very much looking forward to meeting the Governor General's maître d'hôtel from Ottawa! They made me feel like a real VIP and we worked together to set up for what was likely to be the biggest event to be held in Memramcook.

After touring the site, we decided that the VIP lunch would be held in the former chapel of the college. It was old but it was beautiful. Chef Jacques Parent, the executive chef during the LeBlanc mandate, worked on a menu for the Governor General's and Madame LeBlanc's approval and, of course, Monsieur LeBlanc's Acadian specialties were featured. It was decided that the back of the chapel would be turned into a kitchen and, despite the cramped quarters, the entire meal would be prepared in what was formerly known as the sacristy of the church. All the ingredients were purchased locally or in nearby Moncton, Dieppe or Shediac. As for the supplies, our choice for rentals was somewhat limited. We decided instead to rent a large truck and move many of the items that were at the Citadelle in Quebec City to Memramcook. We brought silver and china, crystal and linens. When the loaded truck from Quebec arrived in Memramcook, all hands were on deck for unloading and setting up the room. Before long, the chapel was transformed. It looked as beautiful as the Ballroom at Rideau Hall.

On the day of the event, the excitement could be felt in the air. It was a cool but sunny Fall day, the leaves just starting to change their colours. The Acadian roots of the village were proudly on display. Streets were lined with Acadian flags and homes were decorated with tricolour banners and the yellow star of Acadia. Residents stood outside and watched the parade of limousines as they rounded the bend and headed up the hill towards the college.

Once inside the building, the chapel had to be accessed via a majestic grand staircase. I couldn't help but feel that, after more than 100 years since it was first built, we had played a small part in bringing the old college back to life. When Prime Minister and Madame Chretien arrived, she noticed me standing nearby and I could see through her smile the sense of comfort, and perhaps relief, knowing that we were there.

The luncheon went off without a glitch, despite a few last-minute changes to the seating plan, which our trusted event planner, Sylvie Barsalou, was always prepared for. As delegates were arriving, my team was rolling two extra tables into the room and adding place settings to accommodate unexpected members of delegations. There were also a few VIPs who had confirmed their attendance but did not show up. Again, our team was used to rearranging seating plans and moving place cards, always keeping in mind the sensitivities of international protocol. The luncheon concluded with words of gratitude from Prime Minister Chretien and, before we knew it, the event was over.

As the motorcade returned to Moncton, the peace and serenity of the Memramcook Valley was restored. I recall that many of our staff members watched the departures, breathing a sigh of relief and some shedding a tear knowing that their hard work and long days had concluded with an event which was not only a great success, but which meant the world to Mr. LeBlanc. Afterwards, he thanked us and told us that his words could not express his appreciation and pride. That was sufficient for us.

Richard Legrand, Maître d'hôtel

The LeBlancs with Rideau Hall staff and Culinary Arts and Hospitality students from Memramcook, following the closing luncheon of the 8th Summit of La Francophonie, held at the former Collège St-Joseph, the first francophone university in Eastern Canada, established in 1864. The luncheon was attended by more than 50 Heads of State from francophone countries around the world.
Photo credit: Rideau Hall

THE SOURCE OF WATER

The setting was a formal dinner for a visiting head of state. Shortly after the meal service began, I was pulled aside by a senior member of the Household who scolded me for serving water from a bottle instead of the glass pitchers we traditionally used during formal dinners. Unbeknownst to him, earlier that evening and just prior to the dinner, I was summoned by the security officer from the visiting head of state's delegation who insisted that water had to be served from sealed bottles! It was clear that they did not trust the source of our tap water, something which had never entered my mind! Without further thought, we replaced the crystal pitchers of water with sealed bottles, allowing the security officers to focus their attention on more significant threats, if any.

Richard Legrand, Maître d'hôtel

THE MEANING OF WORDS

I learned early in my career at Rideau Hall that when someone took the time to write a letter, whether it was to extend an invitation, share an opinion or even to express dissatisfaction with a decision, the writer deserved to receive an acknowledgement. I also learned the value of a well-written letter to the person receiving it.

As a teen in high school, I knew that I wanted to pursue a higher level of education. I also knew that a class in typing and Pitman's shorthand could come in handy as a backup plan! Sure enough, in my first job at Rideau Hall, as the clerical assistant to the Administrative Secretary, I spent countless hours sitting in the boss' office, taking dictation in shorthand for letters that often said the same thing but were uniquely different. And, when typed on Government House letterhead, it truly looked like the writer had set everything aside to personally reflect on a reply. My boss, Edmond Joly de Lotbinière, would choose each word carefully and occasionally enter into deep thought, leaving me, an impatient 21-year-old sitting across from him, wondering if he might have dozed off! In the end, the letters were beautiful, and the correspondence almost always ended with the same polite salutation and very best wishes. Little did I know that the letter-writing skills I had painfully acquired during those earlier years, would serve me throughout my career and beyond.

Most of my years at Rideau Hall were spent working in program planning. Each year, we received hundreds of letters and invitations to the Governor General and his or her spouse. The subject matter varied but, for the most part, the letters ranged from official invitations to events and conferences to heartfelt invitations from a grade 3 class or a small community to officially open the Fall Fair. In each case, our program officers would assess the invitation based on a number of criteria including the Governor General's availability, travel requirements, cost, impact, and interest. Quite often, we would combine several invitations for a certain part of the country not yet visited and plan a regional visit which included a number of events. Once approved by the Governor General, it was always a pleasure to contact the person or organization extending the invitation to inform them that their request had been accepted! Unfortunately, there were so many more that had to be declined for practical reasons.

One of the most difficult and challenging times of my career came because of one such letter. It was a last-minute invitation, sent by e-mail, two days before the event, inviting Governor General Adrienne Clarkson to attend a same-sex marriage ceremony at a Church in Toronto. The Reverend Brent Hawkes would preside the ceremony on January 14, 2001. Knowing that Mrs. Clarkson would be away that weekend, I asked our correspondence writer to send the standard "decline letter" with the usual congratulations and best wishes on behalf of the Governor General. The reply was sent by e-mail with a hard copy to follow. The next day, an urgent call from Stewart Wheeler, our Press Secretary, told me that there was a problem. When questioned about the invitation, which I remembered because it had come in at the last minute, I replied that yes, we had received it and that we had simply sent regrets with the usual best wishes. The next morning, most major news outlets were reporting that Adrienne Clarkson had intentionally stepped into the political and controversial debate about same-sex marriage by conveying her best wishes to the couple in question. Parliamentarians of all stripes, religious officials, social groups, community activists and ordinary citizens reacted to the coverage, some supportive but most accusing Madame Clarkson of meddling in government policy and participating in social activism. Despite

Stewart Wheeler's best efforts to explain that "the staff member had merely used standard courteous language to reply to an invitation the Governor General was not able to accept," the general reaction was that "Adrienne Clarkson had overstepped the bounds of her Office" by sending her best wishes to the couple.

The amount of correspondence and phone calls generated by this incident was unprecedented. We hired two additional writers to assist with the volume of letters, some of them quite harsh and critical. I was completely taken aback. For an Office which prides itself with being apolitical, we had unintentionally plunged the Governor General into a hotbed of criticism. In a moment of inattention, I never thought to link the then government's policy on same sex marriage to the possibility that someone would use our standard "best wishes", traditionally sent to any couple getting married, to advance a cause. The incident left me feeling disappointed in myself but also in civil society. I took responsibility for my error in judgement and a few days later, I spoke to Adrienne Clarkson to apologize for the chaos created by our letter. She was bothered by it but was not sorry for the position she was accused of taking. She listened and reassured me that she understood our letter was well-intentioned; however, it also presented an opportunity for critics of the Office and of her personally to use it as a platform for their own positions. I was grateful to her for sharing her view of the situation with me and for reassuring me of her continued faith in my work.

The letter-writing campaign eventually slowed down and, just a few years later, in 2008, I watched as the Reverend Brent Hawkes, the presiding minister at the wedding in 2001, was invested as a Member of the Order of Canada by Governor General Michaëlle Jean, for his achievements as a champion of human rights and social justice.

Gabrielle Lappa

The Globe and Mail, January 16, 2001, Michael Valpy

THE ROYALS

Their Excellencies
the Governor General
and Mrs. Ramon John Hnatyshyn
wish to invite you
to a reception
in honour of
Her Majesty Queen Elizabeth II
on Sunday, July 1st, 1990
at 3:15 p.m.
at Rideau Hall

Invitation card

A SPECIAL GIFT

My first trips on the vice-regal train were as assistant steward to Viscount Willingdon in 1926 and to the Earl of Bessborough, between 1931 and 1935 and later as the steward to Lord Tweedsmuir. We made regular tours across Canada to Vancouver and Victoria in the spring, and to the Maritimes in the fall.

On the morning of May 16, 1939, Their Majesties King George VI and Queen Elizabeth boarded the train at Palais Station in Québec, for an 8,600-mile trip across Canada and then down to Washington and Hyde Park as guests of the President of the United States. The trip lasted a month and we arrived back in Halifax on June 15th.

One morning, the Earl of Sirlie came to tell me that the King and Queen would receive me and my crew of four on board the *Empress of Britain* at 7:30 p.m. to say goodbye. Even though we saw them every day, this was quite an honour for us. I was presented with a set of gold cuff links by the King who told me to wear them, not to leave them in a case on my dressing table! He also mentioned that, when his daughters were older, (the present Queen Elizabeth II was only 13 years old at the time) they would return to Canada and he hoped that I would be around to look after them as well as I had looked after Their Majesties.[10]

Wilfred Notley, C.M., Chief Steward.

Mr. Wilfred Notley, C.M., passed away on March 10th, 2007 in Ottawa.

---

10   Wilfred Notley, Chief Steward, Quote from Employee Reunion Collection, 1992

ROYALTY IN PORTAGE LA PRAIRIE

I was a young RCAF captain when I first arrived at Rideau Hall to serve as the aide-de-camp to Governor General Ramon John Hnatyshyn. I knew there would be long days working for the Commander-in-Chief, especially one who was as active as Ray Hnatyshyn. I started my assignment in September 1994 and had my first day off six months later.

At the beginning and the end of a governor general's mandate, it is traditional for the Queen's representative in Canada to travel to the UK to meet and later bid farewell to Her Majesty the Queen. Although I had only been in my position for a few months, the visit to England fell within my "in-waiting" period so I was responsible for every last detail of the farewell trip. At Her Majesty's request, the visit was to take place at Sandringham Estate, instead of Buckingham Palace, where the Queen normally spends about two months each winter.

We travelled to the UK by RCAF Challenger, landing at Royal Air Force Base Marham where we were met by two Range Rovers. We drove directly to Sandringham (approximately 100 miles north of London) and, to my surprise, we were greeted at the front door by none other than the Queen and Prince Philip. Upon entering the Residence, we were shown into the living room just off the entranceway which I recall being far less formal than many of the rooms at Rideau Hall. Queen Elizabeth the Queen Mother was there as was Princess Anne and a few members of the Royal Household. I was invited by the Queen Mum to sit by her so we could chat. Almost immediately, she turned to me and said "Hello Michael. Now, tell me how my regiments in Canada are doing?" Fortunately, I knew enough to remember that the Queen

Mother was, among others, the Honorary Colonel of The Black Watch (Royal Highland Regiment) of Canada. I responded positively that all her regiments "were doing fine, Ma'am." She then proceeded to ask me if I had ever been to Portage La Prairie in Manitoba. I had, in fact, been there and was curious about what, in Portage La Prairie, had left such an impression. The Queen Mum went on to explain that she had such fond memories of the 1939 Royal Tour of Canada with King George VI, most of which was undertaken by train. She explained that there had been a delay in their schedule, so it was very late into the night when the royal train pulled into a siding outside of Portage La Prairie. They had prepared for bed when, in the dark of the night, they were awakened by knocks on the window of their train car. Pulling open the curtains and looking out the window, the Queen Mother saw a group of people waiving at them in excitement. The Queen Mum went on to explain that, even though she was in her dressing gown, she decided to go to the door to wish them well. On her way there, she realized that she had forgotten something. She returned to her room and put on her tiara! The loyal fans clearly made a lasting impression on the Queen Mum as did she on them!

Lieutenant-General Michael John Hood, C.M.M., CD, was a former aide-de-camp to Governors General Hnatyshyn and LeBlanc, and, more recently, the former commander of the Royal Canadian Air Force.

CARDS WITH THE QUEENS

During the Hnatyshyns' two-day visit to Sandringham at the end of their mandate, the dinners, although fairly intimate, were black tie events with the Queen and Prince Philip, in full regalia. Prior to the dinner and towards the end of each afternoon, everyone would gather in the parlor for a drink and informal chat. Her Majesty would then leave to get changed and everyone had to do the same and be back down in 30 minutes before the Queen returned.

Earlier that afternoon, I found myself having a little free time between lunch and the planned afternoon drinks, having told Mr. and Mrs. Hnatyshyn that I would come and get them just before drinks at 17:00 and brief them on the schedule of events for the evening. I took advantage of the free time to wander around Sandringham and admire the artwork when I heard my name being called. It was the Queen. "Michael, why don't you come and join Mummy and me for cards?" Before I knew it, a folding card table was set up and the Queen, as well as the Queen Mother, attempted to teach me how to play a game called "Patience". I had no idea how the game was played nor was I going to learn because, essentially, both ladies were playing my cards for me!

At the same time, I was very conscious of the fact that Mr. and Mrs. Hnatyshyn were expecting me to brief them at 4:30 in their rooms. As a member of the Canadian Armed Forces and an aide-de-camp, being late or keeping the Boss waiting was not an option, except when one is involved in a card game with two Queens. I attempted to explain to Her Majesty that I would have to excuse myself to brief the Governor

General who was expecting me at 4:30. While contemplating her next move with the cards, and without so much as a glimpse, she replied "Oh, don't worry Michael, they will be fine." Fortunately, the game eventually ended, and I managed to dash upstairs for the meeting, hoping that the Governor General would believe my excuse!

Later that evening, despite the dinner being a formal event, the conversation was not only pleasant but also quite informal. As the dinner drew to an end, the doors opened and in came the royal corgis! The Queen had saved some food on her plate and handed the bits to the dogs. This was also the signal that dinner was over. Her Majesty, the Queen Mother, Mrs. Hnatyshyn and other ladies moved into another room for coffee while the Prince and other male guests, including this young Captain, stayed at the dinner table and enjoyed cigars and scotch!

Lieutenant-General Michael John Hood, C.M.M, CD.

A ROYAL PICNIC

One of the most casual events during the Governor General and Mrs. Hnatyshyn's two-day visit with the Queen and Prince Philip was the picnic lunch. On the second day, following the formal dinner the previous evening, Her Majesty arranged for us to have a casual picnic luncheon with them on the Sandringham estate. Off we went, in the two Land Rovers, with the Queen driving the first one, and Prince Philip and Mr. Hnatyshyn in the second. After a breathtaking drive through the countryside, I spotted what appeared to be a small cabin in the distance. It was near this tiny one room house where the Queen parked the car and proceeded to set up for our picnic lunch.

Prince Phillip started handing me the baskets to bring inside. As Her Majesty was unpacking the basket I had just brought in, she said to me, "Michael, have you been into my buns?" I froze, trying to decipher what exactly she was asking me. I soon learned that someone had opened the basket and broken off a big hunk of bread. Fortunately for me, Prince Philip came to my rescue and responded to Her Majesty's accusation by saying, "Don't be daft. It was me!" His Royal Highness then asked me what time it was, to which I replied that it was close to 11:00 a.m. He immediately pulled out a few shot glasses and filled them with elderberry wine. Without a doubt, a memorable moment in my career!

Lieutenant-General Michael John Hood, C.M.M, CD.

A ROYAL HONOUR

In 1996, prior to departing Rideau Hall at the end of a royal visit by Her Majesty and Prince Phillip, I, along with other members of our staff, were called to the small Drawing Room. Her Majesty thanked everyone for their work and assistance in making the visit a success. She then reached for a small box on a table and presented me with the Medal of the Royal Victorian Order. The Queen congratulated me for all my years of service. I was completely surprised and became very emotional. Her Majesty and Prince Phillip both laughed and said it was time to be happy, not to cry.

It was truly an honour to be able to work for Her Majesty and His Royal Highness each time they were at Rideau Hall. To be honoured for it was not expected but nonetheless appreciated.

Richard Legrand, R.V.M.

SERVICE WITH A SMILE!

In 1967, Centennial year, we had over 60 state visits at Rideau Hall. From June to October, we worked 20-hour days with no time off in between. One delegation would arrive as one was leaving. That year, our staff increased from four footmen to six, just to keep up with the official visits. Many staff members were not able to keep up with the demands of the job and simply left.

The main course for most state visits was rack of lamb, which was served at each table by one footman holding the large meat platter in one hand and a tray with 3 types of sauces on the other. The second footman held a large platter with the vegetables. Guests would then serve themselves and add the sauce of their choice to the plate. Those silver platters were very heavy and even more so when they were filled with food! I have to admit that there were a few occasions when peas fell to the floor or mashed potatoes missed the plate but, fortunately, these occasions were rare, and we did what we could to hide the evidence from the guests!

Unfortunately, the worst food incident happened to one of our footmen on the vice-regal train – with Her Majesty the Queen. When the train came to a sudden stop, the soup bowls slid off the table, with one landing straight onto Her Majesty's lap! We were aghast but, as usual, she was very gracious and laughed about the incident!

Jimmy (Gilles) Carrière, Footman

SAVING THE QUEEN!

The year 1959 was an especially busy one for Mr. Massey. Her Majesty the Queen toured Canada from June 18th to August 1, 1959, covering more than 15,000 miles. The highlight of that visit was the opening of the St. Lawrence Seaway on June 26th in Cornwall, Ontario.

A few days later, during a visit to St. Catharines, Ontario, as Her Majesty was boarding the vice-regal train following an event, the train unexpectedly lurched forward a few feet. It was just enough to throw Her Majesty off balance, causing her to fall backwards. To my surprise, and to everyone's relief, The Queen landed safely in my arms! She graciously thanked me for helping her to which I replied, "It was my pleasure, Your Majesty!" Just another day on the train![11]

Wilfred Notley, C.M.

Wilfred Notley was the Chief Steward on the vice-regal trains for Viscount Willingdon, the Earl of Bessborough, Lord Tweedsmuir, the Earl of Athlone, Viscount Alexander of Tunis, Vincent Massey, General Vanier, and Roland Michener. Photo credit: Joyce Bryant, personal collection

---

11   Wilfred Notley, Chief Steward, Quote from Employee Reunion Collection, 1992

SHE REMEMBERED ME!

In 1973, I was informed, by letter from Government House, that I was to be appointed a Member of the Order of Canada and that, when Her Majesty the Queen was going to be in Ottawa in August, I was going to be included on a short list of those to be invested by The Queen herself.

My big day was August 2nd. My wife and I left early for Government House that morning. Having never missed a train in 42 years, I wanted to be sure to not spoil my record on this very special occasion! We arrived at the appointed hour and were met by an Aide-de-Camp who escorted us to the Ambassadors' Room for a briefing and then to the Ballroom. Shortly after, we all arose to a fanfare as Her Majesty the Queen entered. Following the playing of the Royal Anthem, the investiture started.

The Secretary to the Governor General, Mr. Esmond Butler, read my citation: "For distinguished service under two sovereigns and eight Governors General". While the Queen was pinning the Order of Canada insignia onto my jacket, she thanked me for all the royal tours during which I had looked after her and she reminded me of the day, 14 years earlier, in St. Catharines, Ontario, when I caught her in my arms, as the train lurched forward while she was boarding. She remarked, "Thank you so much for looking after us during our visits to Canada, and for rescuing me that day!" I wasn't sure if it was the fall or the rescuer that left an impression on Her Majesty but, regardless, her recollection of the event was special.[12]

Wilfred Notley, Chief Steward

---

12   Wilfred Notley, Chief Steward, Quote from Employee Reunion Collection, 1992

THE PRINCESS OF WALES –
A FINAL FAREWELL

It was June 1983 when Their Royal Highnesses the Prince and Princess of Wales visited Rideau Hall as part of an 18-day tour to Canada. They had wed two years earlier and were relatively new parents to the young Prince William. Whether you were a royal watcher or just fascinated by the frenzy, the royal couple was met with the warmest of welcomes everywhere they went.

At Rideau Hall, the Schreyers invited staff members to gather in the Front Foyer for the arrival of the Prince and Princess. It was an unwritten tradition that, when state visitors arrived, they would be greeted by the staff as they entered the Residence and then introduced to members of the Governor General's Household. The entourage accompanying the royal couple would, in turn, be introduced to the Governor General and his or her family, and then escorted to their rooms.

As Their Royal Highnesses walked through the front doors that day, they were greeted by a warm, welcoming applause. Princess Diana, once described as the most photographed woman in the world, was strikingly beautiful and yet understated. The royal couple represented all that the Crown could be, particularly for a younger generation.

Fourteen years later, in August 1997, news of the death of Princess Diana shocked the world. It was a Saturday evening, and, by Sunday morning, I was making calls to funeral homes and driving around Ottawa looking for a condolence book large enough to hold many signatures. Needless to say, no one was prepared for such an event.

Fortunately, our calligrapher, Barbara Lovelace, found beautiful albums at a local papery that could be taken apart, with pages added or removed as needed.

Within hours, the staff had set up a signature table with flowers alongside a large photo of the Princess that someone had arranged to have enlarged and framed in record time. A press release went out announcing that the Residence would be open for those who wished to sign the book of condolences. That same afternoon, we watched as streams of people walked up the long drive to Rideau Hall to sign the book, express their feelings and even shed a tear. Along the front of the Residence, mounds of floral bouquets, single roses and teddy bears accumulated. For the next few days, the line-up of people, young and old, wound its way down the drive. Our staff members took turns assisting those in line, keeping them informed of the approximate wait time, and listening to their stories.

Their Royal Highnesses, the Prince and Princess of Wales, arriving at Rideau Hall in June 1983. (Photo: personal collection)

After a few long days and following the funeral services for the Princess in London, the signature books were closed. The front pages were calligraphed and the individual sheets, filled with the names and heartfelt sentiments of Canadians, were assembled into books and forwarded to Buckingham Palace. The many bouquets of still fresh flowers were delivered to local Residences for seniors and the teddy bears were dropped off at the Children's Hospital, just as Princess Diana would have wanted.

Gabrielle Lappa

INSPIRATIONS

ONE OF A KIND

It was the Rt. Hon. Vincent Massey, the first Canadian to serve as Governor General from 1952 to 1959, who first "planted the seed" for a Canadian Honours System. Mr. Massey had spent much of his time in Office travelling to every corner of the country, promoting Canadian unity and identity. Throughout the mandate, much research and groundwork were done on the proposal, assisted by Joyce Bryant, his trusted secretary. A few years later, when Prime Minister Lester B. Pearson was elected in 1963, he fully supported Mr. Massey's proposal and it was decided that Canada's Centennial celebration in 1967 would be the perfect opportunity to announce the uniquely Canadian system of honours and the creation of the Order of Canada.

Working for the Office of the Governor General and the Chancellery of Honours meant that we would often meet and speak with outstanding Canadians who were being recognized and honoured for their service and contributions to our country. In all or most cases, lives were changed because of these individuals and they truly deserved the gratitude of a nation when they were presented with our national honours and awards by the Governor General.

Nothing is more impressive than a medal or insignia worn proudly by the person who earned the award. I was fortunate to work at the Chancellery with the gentleman who, at the request of Prime Minister Lester B. Pearson, was asked to design one of Canada's most beautiful insignia – the Order of Canada.

Following the end of WWII, young Flight Sergeant Bruce Beatty returned to Ottawa where he began working as a graphic designer with the Directorate of Ceremonial at National Defence Headquarters. Over the years, Bruce had created many of Canada's medals and decorations for the military. Suffice it to say that Bruce was more than a little surprised when he was summoned to the Prime Minister's office at the Langevin Building to meet with Lester B. Pearson.

It was during this meeting that the Prime Minister shared his wish to establish a new national Order and tasked Bruce with the design of its insignia, giving him carte blanche. The only proviso was that the ribbon was to be the same colours and proportions of the newly minted Canadian flag. Sworn to secrecy, Bruce recalled how the PM told him, "Don't tell anyone, not even your commanding officer, or your wife."

Leaving the Prime Minister's office that day, Bruce had a lot to process in very little time. It was while walking along Elgin Street that cold Friday afternoon in November, on his way to the Beaver Barracks (home of the Warrant Officers' and Sergeants' Mess) that inspiration struck! Bruce was a great storyteller and he often recounted this moment, describing how it had started to snow gently with large white snowflakes landing on him and on the sidewalk before him. He thought to himself, "What could be more Canadian than a snowflake? They are all unique and different." The snowflake became the inspiration for the new insignia for future recipients of the Order of Canada, to which Bruce always added "It was my Eureka moment!" A short time later, Bruce presented the Prime Minister with his final design: a six-armed snowflake with a maple leaf in the centre. And the rest, as they say, is history.

Kristina Jensen, Order of Canada Analyst, Chancellery of Honours, 20 years

Captain Bruce Beatty, who continued to assist the Chancellery with national ceremonies long after his retirement, was honoured for his contribution to the nation when he was appointed a Member of the Order of Canada on April 20, 1990. Personal collection: Danielle Dougall

THE DEFINITION OF BRAVERY

"The hope of courage lies in every heart, together with the fear that we will fail. When the test came, you did not fail."[13]

The Rt. Hon. Roméo LeBlanc,
Presentation of Bravery Decorations, June 23, 1995

I learned about the tremendous courage of people of all ages when I first started working at the Chancellery of Honours in 1977, during the Léger mandate. As the Assistant Director responsible for the national Bravery Decorations program, we would review hundreds of nominations each year for individuals who, without concern for their own safety, did not hesitate to risk their lives to help others in distress. With almost every new case, we read about explosions, lost limbs, disfiguring burns, animal attacks, and individuals jumping into rushing torrents of icy waters to help others, many times complete strangers. The accounts of some of the incidents were unimaginable. Meeting the award recipients at Rideau Hall was the ultimate reward.

Anyone can nominate a deserving individual for a Decoration for Bravery. The degree of risk and persistence of the individual, and knowing that they might be injured or killed, determines which of the three levels would be awarded. The Medal of Bravery recognizes acts in hazardous circumstances; the Star of Courage, acts of conspicuous courage in circumstances of great peril; and the Cross of Valour,

---

13   Speech delivered by the Rt. Hon. Roméo Leblanc, Presentation of Bravery Decorations, June 23, 1995

the highest civilian award for bravery, recognizes acts of the most conspicuous courage in circumstances of extreme peril. This award is listed just below the Victoria Cross in the order of precedence for Canadian decorations and medals. Their stories were inspiring and, at times, inconceivable.

Each eligible nomination is reviewed by the Canadian Decorations Advisory Committee, made up of representatives from different fields including fire, police, medical, air and transportation safety as well as select government departments. Each year, approximately 100 recipients of the award are recognized and honoured for their courage and bravery at a ceremony presided by the Governor General two to three times per year.

As difficult as it was to read the heart-wrenching police reports and witness statements for many of the nominations, the most difficult was watching the next-of-kin of posthumous recipients during the ceremonies, many reliving the final moments of their loved ones.

The period leading up to each ceremony was a time when most of the Chancellery and the Rideau Hall team came together to ensure that all the details were covered. Arrangements had to be made for the recipients and their families, many sometimes travelling from far or from remote parts of the country, often their first time in the Nation's Capital. Medals were prepared and ribbons hand-sewn on each, programs were printed, scenarios with minute-by-minute details were prepared by the aide-de-camp, and the executive chef and his team were busy preparing for a luncheon for 200 or more guests. On the morning of the event, it was heart warming to watch as the recipients and their families came off the chartered buses and entered Rideau Hall. We could sense the anxiety and emotions running high, sometimes even amongst our own staff who were anxious to meet the award recipients whose files they had worked on. Not surprisingly, the recurring sentiment amongst the award recipients was that they did not see themselves as heroes and that "anyone would have done the same thing." Although it is impossible to know how we would react in the face of danger should we be confronted with situations similar to those we heard about at the ceremonies, it was always humbling to see and hear the reactions of the medal recipients and of the audience when the citations were read.

Among the most moving presentations were those to children who didn't hesitate to "do the right thing" sometimes not even understanding the potential dangers they faced.

Some of the most memorable cases for me included Julius, a 5-year-old, who made angry noises like "the Hulk" to chase away a bear that had gripped his younger sister by her jacket.

Jean-Paul, 6, was with his father on a snowmobile when his dad was severely injured. The little boy set off for help, retracing the snowmobile tracks. After getting lost, he continued to trek through deep snow until he reached a highway and flagged down a passing motorist. At 7 years of age, Marie-Hélène rescued her younger brother after he had fallen into a river. Hearing his cries, she went down the steep slope and took his hand but fell in herself. Supporting her brother with one hand, she clutched the shore until her mother heard their screams and pulled them out. Nicholas, a 6-year-old and his 20-month-old brother were playing in their farmhouse while their parents milked the cows. When he smelled smoke, Nick brought his brother upstairs and called 911, then crawled 30 m to safety through thick smoke, carrying his brother on his back. And there were so many more.

Despite the sombre moments when the citations are read during the ceremonies, there are also a few surprises. For example, when came the time for the presentation to a young mother from the Yukon who had rescued her two small children from a grizzly bear attack in their yard, the gasps of surprise and disbelief could be heard throughout the room when a slight woman, of fairly small stature, walked to the front of the Ballroom and stood shyly as her citation was read. A well-deserved standing ovation followed!

Occasionally, we are called upon to perform our own "rescues" although none deserving of a medal! During one of the luncheons following the ceremony, a colleague approached me and whispered in my ear that the medal belonging to one of the recipients had fallen off his jacket and into the toilet bowl. Fortunately, the medal was fished out and we were able to have a replacement ribbon sewn onto the sparkling clean medal and returned to the slightly embarrassed recipient by the time the lunch was over!

In everyone's career, there is at least one event that stretches us to the limit. In my case, it was the nomination, review and awarding of 201 Bravery decorations to the men involved in a rescue operation for 26 miners in one of the most tragic mining disasters in Canadian history. The Westray Mine explosion occurred on May 9th, 1992, in Pictou County, Nova Scotia. The award ceremony was for 180 of the recipients, the largest group to receive the Decoration for Bravery for a single incident since the beginning of the program in 1972.

Prior to the presentations, each nomination was reviewed to ensure that the criteria were met. Naturally, emotions, politics, and unions all play an important role in the tragic details of such an event and the review process by the Decorations Advisory Committee was an onerous task. Our team worked countless hours gathering reports and witness statements for each of the 201 recipients. Almost three years later, on November 28th, 1994, 180 of these heroes were recognized for their selfless acts of bravery during a nationally televised ceremony which took place in Stellarton, Nova Scotia, home to many of the victims and recipients of the awards. The remaining 21 recipients received their awards at a later ceremony presented by the Lieutenant Governor of Nova Scotia in Halifax.

Danielle Dougall, Assistant Director, Decorations and Medals, 29 years of service.

HEROES AMONG US – STELLARTON, NOVA SCOTIA

I will never forget one of the most moving and yet challenging events of my time at Rideau Hall. It was a Bravery award ceremony to honour 180 of the 201 men who were involved in a rescue operation for 26 miners in the Westray Mine explosion. This tragic disaster touched all or most of the residents in the Pictou County communities of Nova Scotia.

It was decided that the ceremony honouring these brave men and their families would be held in their community of Stellarton, population of less than 5,000 people. We were tasked with setting up an event which was solemn, dignified, and which would bring the same Rideau Hall standards to this small town in Nova Scotia. Our Bravery Decorations team at the Chancellery of Honours worked diligently to ensure that all the recipients and/or their families were invited. Emotions ran high at both ends of the phone lines and we were determined to make the experience for these Canadians as special as if they were travelling to Rideau Hall. This was always very important to our team and I think our guests appreciated it, no matter where we were in Canada.

We had to start from scratch. The venues which could accommodate this number of guests were limited in Stellarton. Also, the CBC wanted to broadcast the ceremony "live", so we had a few challenges. In the end, the chosen location was the Sharon St. John United Church, a beautiful old church on one of the main streets in this small community. The reception would be held in the school gym close by.

While our colleagues at the Chancellery focused on the recipients and the details of the ceremony, my greatest concern was having enough supplies to accommodate everyone and to transform the gym for the reception. I decided to start with the flowers. Off I went to the only little flower shop in Stellarton and informed the young lady at the desk that I needed thousands of white Casablanca lilies. She stared at me with a frozen look and said she did not have any at the moment! I can't even imagine what she was thinking! Of course, we worked together on options for the church and for transforming the gym and, in the end, the florists did a darn good job! The basketball nets were tucked away, and the room was draped in flags and flowers. It all looked beautiful.

The day of the ceremony was cold but sunny. Governor General Ray Hnatyshyn arrived in Stellarton and busloads of recipients, guests and members of the media came from different parts of the province and the country. As guests entered the church and were greeted by members of our staff, the feelings of sadness, nervousness and even reluctance on the part of the recipients were tangible. All of them had lost family members, friends and co-workers. They did not feel that they were brave, and many felt that perhaps their efforts should not be rewarded because they had not succeeded in saving many lives. In our eyes, they were all heroes.

The award ceremony in the church was somber and moving, paying tribute to the men, dead and alive, who had been involved in the tragedy. The Director of Honours at the time, Mary de Bellefeuille-Percy was the master of ceremonies and gave the event the dignity it deserved. The Maritime group, 'Men of the Deeps,' sang during the ceremony and brought tears to everyone's eyes. Millions of Canadians from coast to coast to coast watched the ceremony on television.

Following the presentation, everyone moved into the school gym to relax and enjoy the reception. Then the storm hit. It started to rain, then freezing rain, then snow. The roads turned to ice and the bus loads of guests could not leave. Everyone was stuck in the gym. Our staff worked hard to assist the guests, provide updates and serve whatever refreshments remained. They were all so appreciative and grateful. Fortunately, by nightfall, the temperature increased, reducing the freezing rain, and allowing the buses to leave with the guests. The Governor General headed for the airport and, for those of us who could not get out that evening, we doubled up in the only motel in Stellarton which, I think, was owned by the Mayor! There were mattresses in the hallways and the small coffee shop quickly ran out of coffee. The Men of the Deeps entertained us in the pub with their East Coast music well into the early hours and we were finally able to relax after a few long days of preparation and hard work. In the end, the event was memorable in so many ways, not only for the Bravery award recipients and their families but also for those of us who worked together to make the event special for them.

Richard Legrand, Maître d'hôtel

THE "VOICE" OF RIDEAU HALL

During everyone's career, there is at least one person who mentors and inspires us to do our very best. In my case, it was Mary de Bellefeuille-Percy who was the Director of Honours at the Chancellery during most of my time there. Often referred to as the "voice of Rideau Hall," Mary presided over most of the awards ceremonies, many of them televised or taped so that Canadians were able to watch family members and friends being honoured for their bravery, their contributions and their achievements. With a warm and steady voice, Mary would welcome the guests on behalf of the Governor General and read the citations describing the actions or achievements of each recipient. Her steady and reassuring voice would help to calm, as much as possible, the nerves of those standing at the front of the Ballroom waiting to receive their award. Like all the staff at Rideau Hall, Mary felt that the presentation of Decorations for Bravery was the most touching and sometimes emotionally difficult ceremony and she made it a point to always meet with the recipients prior to the presentation to assure them that they were in good hands and that all would be fine.

The ceremonies were then followed by a beautiful reception and buffet luncheon for the recipients and their guests. It was here that everyone could finally relax and enjoy the rest of the day. Mary would walk around the room and chat with the guests, often drawn to the younger ones who, with their spontaneous remarks or occasional cries during the ceremonies, would often add a moment of laughter and levity to an otherwise serious event. On this particular day, spotting a small boy who had sat patiently throughout the almost two-hour ceremony with his parents, Mary approached the family to chat and discovered that the little guy was restless and hungry. While the buffet was still being set up in the Tent Room, and with the parents' approval, Mary took the child by the hand and lead him into the stately room where long tables with different foods and deserts were quickly being set up by the team of chefs. Eyes wide open, the little guy filled his plate to overflowing. With Mary by his side, and clutching his plate, he returned to the reception room to see his parents, both vegetarian, who were stunned to see the plate loaded with meat!

Highly regarded by the five governors general she served as well as by her colleagues and staff, Mary had a natural elegance that endeared her to many of the award recipients she met prior to or after each ceremony, including one of Canada's most respected songwriters and poet, Leonard Cohen. While preparing to read the citations for the Order of Canada ceremony during which Mr. Cohen was to receive the insignia of Companion of the Order from the Right Honourable Adrienne Clarkson, Mary had an inkling that Mr. Cohen might prefer not to be referred to as a "ladies' man." She altered a few words during the reading of the text, which pleased Mr. Cohen greatly. The next day, Mary received a lovely bouquet of roses from none other than Leonard Cohen who was, as Mary described him, a true gentleman! We were more excited than she was!

Throughout her career at Rideau Hall, Mary's dedication and steadfast contributions to the awards ceremonies and her quiet leadership behind the scenes were always appreciated, not only by those who met her, but also by those who served with her.

Danielle Dougall, Assistant Director, Chancellery of Honours, 29 years of service.

Mary de Bellefeuille-Percy, Director of Honours with Danielle Dougall, Assistant Director, Decorations and Medals. Mary passed away in November 2006, just months after her retirement. Photo credit: Danielle Dougall

WITH A GLOWING HEART

He first sang for Governor General Georges Vanier at Rideau Hall in 1965. Fifty-five years later, Garth Hampson continues to inspire national pride each time he sings "O Canada" at an event for Canadians. Although not an employee of Rideau Hall, Garth was considered a member of the Rideau Hall family.

As one of the last RCMP officers to have patrolled the Arctic by dogsled, Garth assisted, saved, inspired, and even entertained Canadians from coast to coast to coast. In 1964, he transferred to Ottawa from Alberta and joined the RCMP Concert Band as the lead vocalist until he retired from the Forces in 1989. Since then, Garth has continued to share his time and his magnetic voice both at Rideau Hall as well as with numerous other organizations.

During Order of Canada ceremonies, Garth watched many people he had met throughout his own career receive the national honour. Bill Lyall from Cambridge Bay in Nunavut received the Order of Canada in 2003 for his work with the Arctic Cooperative. One of ten children, he belonged to a youth group that Garth had founded in Yellowknife. Bill had been in a residential school and Garth was a role model and a mentor for him and for others. Many years later, when Bill received the Order of Canada for his work with the Cooperative and other successful contributions, he immediately recognized Garth at the front of the Ballroom, singing the national anthem and adding dignity and pride to what was probably one of the proudest moments for the distinguished Canadians being honoured.

Among Garth's favorite ceremonies was the presentation of Decorations for Bravery which recognizes people who risked their lives trying to save or protect others. Like many staff members at Rideau Hall, this is the ceremony that often brings tears as well as the loudest applause for the recipients who range in ages from five to ninety-five! Unfortunately, almost every ceremony includes one or two posthumous recipients. As difficult as it is for the family receiving the award on behalf of the deceased, it is also a fitting way for Canada to recognize its heroes.

Former Governors General who came to know Garth, first for his voice and then for his generous smile and personality, often greeted him as a long-lost friend. Following the 100th anniversary ceremony at the Vimy Memorial in France, which Garth attended as part of the Veterans' Affairs contingent, he was "the most popular guy in the group" when former Governor General Michaëlle Jean found out he was there and ran over to see him!

Governor General David Johnston presenting the Queen Elizabeth II Diamond Jubilee Medal to Garth Hampson at Rideau Hall. Photo credit: Rideau Hall

Over the years, Garth also acquired the unofficial title of "Candy Man" at Rideau Hall. Before each ceremony, as guests entered the Ballroom to take their seats, many for the first time, he loved standing at the back of the room, watching their expressions as they walked into the magnificent room. As the staff members fluttered about taking care of the guests and ensuring that all was in order, Garth would often reach into his pocket and slip a Werther's candy into our hand, supplied by his loving wife, Eleanor. In fact, during a visit to the Beaumont Hamel battlefield site in France, one of the Canadian tour guides working there approached Garth and asked, "where's my candy?" She had previously been a tour guide at Rideau Hall and remembered him well!

From the events staff to the ladies in the coat room, Garth was a favorite for everyone. Throughout the years, he received the Queen's Jubilee Medals and was among the first to receive the Sovereign's Medal for Volunteers and the Vice Regal Commendation for long-term and outstanding service to the Office of the Queen's representative, nominated, of course, by the staff at Rideau Hall.

When his longtime friend Joyce Bryant passed away at 94 years of age, herself an employee of Rideau Hall for more than 40 years, Garth sang at her funeral, closing the event as he had done so many times before at Rideau Hall, but this time with one of Joyce's favorite songs by Dame Vera Lynn, "We'll Meet Again." The church was filled with her friends, many of them from her Rideau Hall family.

Gabrielle Lappa with Brad Hampson

Throughout his career and well into retirement, Garth Hampson sang the national anthem as part of ceremonies at Rideau Hall during the mandates of eleven Governors General and over the course of 55 years.
Photo credit: Rideau Hall

TRANSITIONS

"When we were privileged to take up Residence at Rideau Hall in January 1990, both of us were immediately struck by its beauty and moved by the deep historic significance this edifice has for all Canadians. We felt then, and believe even more strongly now, that Rideau Hall should represent the best of Canada – past and present – to visitors."[14]

The Rt. Hon Ramon John Hnatyshyn and Mrs. Gerda Hnatyshyn

The Ballroom at Rideau Hall Photo credit: Gene Hattori

---

14   The Rt. Hon. Ramon John Hnatyshyn and Mrs. Gerda Hnatyshyn, Rideau Hall, Canada's Living Heritage, Ottawa, 1994, p.ix

A NATION MOURNED

It was on a cold March morning that General Vanier passed away. His family, together for the first time in twenty years, would accompany him to Québec with the vice-regal trains. Following the Requiem Mass at the Basilica in Ottawa, the coffin was taken to Union Station on Wellington Street. For the first time, our dear boss would not be in rail car #1 but in a separate rail car. With a Royal Salute of 21 guns, the train slowly pulled out of the station for the General's final journey to Québec. Upon arrival, the coffin was taken to its resting place at the Citadelle.

Madame Vanier returned to Ottawa and, approximately one month later, she would bid farewell to Ottawa as the train pulled out for her new home in Montréal. Her Excellency presented me with a signed photograph. Both of us had tears in our eyes, as she asked me if I would accept something personal belonging to His Excellency. I was offered his signature silk white scarf which she placed in my hands, clasping them in hers with affection. As I left the sitting room, I thought of what journalist Peter Newman had said that day – "How long since we, as a nation, have cried."[15]

Wilfred Notley, C.M., Steward (Viscount Willingdon, Earl of Bessborough, Lord Tweedsmuir, Earl of Athlone, Viscount Alexander of Tunis, Massey, Vanier, Michener)

---

15   Wilfred Notley, C.M., Employee Reunion Collection, 1992

CHANGES

For staff at Rideau Hall, each new mandate brings expected change. With time, the modernization of traditions, protocols and practices becomes inevitable. When I first started working there, most of the staff members at Rideau Hall were single. We lived in the Residence and our work was our life. My colleagues were my family. New staff members were usually hired through word of mouth or because we knew someone that might be good for the position. Loyalty and discretion were high on the list of mandatory requirements for the positions. And in my case, the suit fit! Although there were occasional disagreements amongst the staff, and perhaps a bit of drama like in the soap operas, for the most part, we all worked with a common goal which was to serve the Office and its occupants.

Somewhere in the late 80s, there was a movement to increase awareness of the Office and the need to make the institution more relevant to Canadians. With this modernization came an increase in staff, a dedicated planning and communications team and changes in the decision- making process which involved so many more people. Cost wise, everything increased – more guests, more public events, and less budget, managed by more administrative staff. We were always conscious of cost, but this rarely influenced the result. The demands on the Governors General and their families were also increasing and, for the most part, residents understood that Rideau Hall should exemplify the best of all things Canadian. However, like all government institutions and departments, the trend of "doing more with less" became the direction at Rideau Hall. With the arrival of each new Governor

General, priorities and themes changed. Like Buckingham Palace, Rideau Hall was changing with the times and the once solid stone walls of the Residence became more transparent. For those of us who had been part of the team for so many years, we had to adapt. Despite these changes, the loyalty and commitment of the long-serving staff to the occupants remained steady. The incumbents we worked for knew our strengths and they had faith in us. We always found ways to make things happen seamlessly.

Time also brought organizational changes. The kitchen staff, pantry and housekeepers had always worked as three independent teams, coming together to deliver, like a well-oiled machine. At one point, these three groups merged to become part of a hospitality team under the direction of an experienced manager who brought new ideas and management skills which, I must say, were becoming necessary, while respecting the traditions and dignity of the institution. Where last minute changes at events were unlikely in the past, the introduction of technology and faster communication forced us to adapt to ever-changing scenarios. We had to learn to be better prepared for changes – just like always having three sets of cutlery, linens, dishes and glasses on hand...one set on the tables, one set being cleaned and one in the cupboard – just in case! Throughout it all and in all cases, it was experience, commitment, and common sense that carried us through so many memorable but also stressful times. Looking back, I realize how fortunate I was to have been part of a team of individuals who went beyond their jobs and to whom loyalty and dedication where second nature.

Richard Legrand, Maître d'hôtel

PASSAGES

I was hired to be Mr. Massey's valet long before he was appointed as Governor General. My wife, Anna, and I took care of the Residence in Port Hope as well as Mr. Massey's personal needs. I had always had a sense of the importance of my job since Mr. Massey frequently entertained a number of very distinguished guests and he was highly appreciative of efficiency on the part of his staff. My duties at Government House would be the same but, from now on, I was solely responsible for taking care of the Governor General and of his personal needs.

In late January of 1952, the announcement of Vincent Massey's appointment as Governor General of Canada appeared in every morning and evening paper in the country. He had travelled to England in November to visit with his son Hart and was still there when the announcement was made. We felt tremendously proud for him, that he had been chosen to represent the Crown in this country. No other man, we were quite sure, could have been a better choice for the first Canadian to fill the post. Just a few days later, on February 6th, the papers carried the unexpected and shocking news that King George VI had died suddenly and that his young daughter, Princess Elizabeth, was to be proclaimed Queen. Vincent Massey's departure for Canada was delayed. He attended the state funeral on February 14th and, two days later, flew to Canada to take on his new duties.

For the first few days, Mr. Massey spoke largely of the preparations we would have to handle, of the move to Ottawa and of arrangements to be made at Government House. At one point, he produced a large tin box containing a Governor General's uniform which had been given to him by Lady Tweedsmuir, whose husband had filled the post from 1935-1940. I had to look the clothing over carefully and become familiar with the correct way of wearing it, using a photo of Lord Tweedsmuir as a guide.

On February 28th, Mr. Massey arrived in Ottawa by train, wearing formal morning dress with a black top hat. As the train approached the Union Station, we could see a portion of the crowds that had braved a biting wind to welcome Mr. Massey to the city. Prime Minister St. Laurent was the first to board the train, to warmly shake the hand of Mr. Massey and officially welcome him to the city. A few minutes later, Mr. Massey and his family, the Prime Minister, and others in the party, stepped from the coach onto the red-carpeted platform to meet the members of the Cabinet. It was indeed an historic occasion. The Right Honourable Vincent Massey was the first Canadian to break the tradition of the Office by becoming Canada's eighteenth and first native-born Governor General.

The years flew by and, five years later, on Monday, September 14, 1957, Vincent Massey said his goodbyes to the staff he had come to know so well. To all of them, he expressed his sincere thanks for their devotion to their work. I recall thinking that, at that moment, he looked very tired and sad. He had loved Government House and had enjoyed his work there very much; it was not easy for him to tear away, either from his office or from the members of his staff, for their sincerity and loyalty had been very highly valued.

The following morning, and the last day of the mandate, the staff at Government House lined up inside the main entrance, waiting for Mr. Massey to appear. Fifteen minutes later, he made his familiar entrance into the foyer for the last time. Suddenly, his leaving struck everyone with full force. There were many handshakes, but few words were spoken; many of the staff were overcome with tears. Nobody wanted him to leave, for all felt that their own years at Rideau Hall had been remarkable ones. All knew that the satisfaction and pleasure they had found in their work had been but reflections of the dignity and success he had conferred upon his own.

Before Mr. Massey entered the waiting limousine, the staff came outside to say good-bye once more and to wish him good health, long life, and a desirable rest. The party left for Union Station and, for Vincent Massey, the heavy but honourable Office that had drawn to this Residence Canadians of distinction in every line of endeavor was but a memory.

Union Station was packed with people who had come for the farewell. Mr. Massey was met by the Prime Minister, members of the Cabinet, the military and civic officials, and more members of the staff. Here again, there were many tearful friends. Accompanied by the Prime Minister and Mrs. Diefenbaker, he boarded the special train which was to take Mr. Massey to Port Hope, where he would spend the rest of his life quietly in the comforting rooms and peaceful gardens of his beloved Batterwood House. An hour later, the new Governor General, General Georges Vanier, arrived to be sworn in."[16]

Miroslav Mircha, Valet to the Rt. Hon. Vincent Massey (deceased)

---

16   Miroslav Mircha, Employee Reunion Collection, 1992

A FOND FAREWELL

Departure and arrival days are rarely forgotten. The toughest part of my job at Rideau Hall came with the end of each mandate. It was a ritual, tenants moving out and new tenants moving in, with sometimes little more than a few hours in between. It was also a time to say farewell to an individual, a couple or a family for whom you had become not only a dedicated employee but, at times, also a confidant and a protector.

The transition period was filled with changes and demands which could become overwhelming and emotionally draining. Despite this, we knew that, even though we felt sadness as we said our goodbyes at 10:00 a.m., we needed to be ready and smiling at 2:00 p.m. because the new Governor General and his or her family were arriving...and they needed our support.

Those of us who were there when the Rt.Hon. Jeanne Sauvé and her husband, Maurice, left Rideau Hall at the end of the mandate will always remember the tears and emotions that day. The staff was very fond of Madame Sauvé, almost in a protective way. She had been ill prior to arriving at Rideau Hall and her installation as Governor General had been delayed by a number of months to allow her the time to recover. Despite this setback, she arrived at Rideau Hall determined to carry out her duties as the first female Governor General of Canada. And though many of us worried about her, she never faltered. She brought to Rideau Hall a level of elegance and grace, surpassed only by her appreciation and respect for those around her.

On the last day of the mandate, as Their Excellencies came down from their private quarters and walked towards the front of the Residence, staff had formed a long human chain from the central hallway to the front door. Overwhelmed by emotions, the tears that had been wiped away before coming down could no longer be controlled. They hugged staff, slowly moving towards the front door where the chauffeur awaited, as always. I was the last person in line before they exited the Residence, and as Madame Sauvé approached me with tears in her eyes, she leaned over and whispered to me "Richard, you were my angel."

As the car pulled away and the Sauvés left for Montréal, the heavy wooden doors closed behind them and I saw colleagues wiping away their tears, as they quietly went back to their work. Within hours, the Rt. Hon. Ramon John Hnatyshyn would arrive with his family and they needed to be welcomed into their new home.

Richard Legrand, Maître d'hôtel

MEMORIES, MOMENTS
AND MISHAPS

WALTER GRETZKY,
PROUD CANADIAN, PROUD DAD

For the last seven years of my career, I worked as the Director of Honours with a team of employees who ran, with dedication and precision, the programs that make up our Canadian Honours System. The nomination process, the review of the files by various committees and the presentation of the awards, whether at Rideau Hall, the Citadelle or in the recipients' own communities, require an enormous amount of planning and processing. The end results are always rewarding. It is also at the end of this process, before or after the actual presentation ceremony, when we often get to meet and speak with the recipients. In the case of the Order of Canada, a black-tie dinner follows the investiture ceremony during which staff members are asked to host individual tables. Conversations are always interesting, entertaining and sometimes revealing.

During one of these evenings, I was seated next to Walter Gretzky, father of the famous Wayne Gretzky, who was appointed to the Order for his outstanding contributions to numerous charitable and non-profit organizations. To my right was the multi-talented Canadian musician and composer, Paul Shaffer, originally from Thunder Bay, Ontario. For over 30 years, Paul was the musical director and band leader for the well-known late-night talk show from New York City, The Late Show with David Letterman. In addition to his musical achievements, Paul was recognized for his major contributions to Lakehead University in Thunder Bay and for showcasing Canadian talent at every opportunity.

The evening was magical as usual, especially for the recipients who, more than anything, seem to enjoy meeting and chatting with other outstanding Canadians from all walks of life. Walter Gretzky, clearly a kind and thoughtful person, asked almost everyone he met if they had children who liked hockey. If so, he pulled out the little notepad and pen he carried in his jacket pocket and asked the person to write the names of their children and their address so that he could send them an autographed photo of his son, Wayne. At the end of the evening, when guests were leaving the Ballroom, I watched as Walter went around to the footmen who had served the dinner to thank them and, of course, ask if they would like a signed photo of his son! He was one of the last guests to leave the room, chatting with staff and entertaining them with his stories.

Just a few months later, two autographed photos of Wayne Gretzky arrived at our home for our sons, with a kind note to me from Walter Gretzky, proud member of the Order of Canada but, more importantly, proud Dad!

Walter Gretzky and Paul Shaffer received the Order of Canada from the Rt. Hon. Michaëlle Jean in 2008. Photo credit: Joanne MacDonald, O.C.

DOILIES FOR DESSERT

The formalities that are part of black-tie dinners at Rideau Hall are always impressive and an important part of the experience for the guests. For one of these formal evenings, the pastry chef had prepared a lovely peach melba for dessert. It was customary to serve this in a fine bowl that sat atop a very thin cloth doily on a plate. Unfortunately, one of the guests thought that the tiny, starched doily was part of the dessert...so he ate it! As we watched from our stations in the Ballroom, we could not believe our eyes! Not certain whether we should approach the gentleman to try to avert a possible incident, we watched him reach for his champagne and wash it down, like a biscuit. Fortunately, the meal ended shortly thereafter, and the gentleman left the room rather quickly. Unfortunately for us, we no longer had a complete set of doilies!

Gilles (Jimmy) Carrière, Footman

FINGER BOWL SOUP

The event was a formal state luncheon for the president of a small country. Towards the end of these VIP luncheons or dinners, it was standard practice to use finger bowls, just before the dessert course, for guests to rinse their fingers. One of the greenhouse employees would come into the back serving room to put colourful flower petals in each finger bowl before they were placed in front of the guests.

During this particular meal, we watched as one of the guests took the finger bowl with his two hands and drank from it. But this was not the worst of it. On his way out of the dining room, we noticed a small petal still clinging to the corner of the guest's mouth. As footmen, we always tried to maintain a serious face but this time it was hard to hide our laughter. Her Excellency noticed our smirks and her eyes warned us that we had better "smarten up!". Fortunately, she also had a laugh when she learned of the incident from the maître d'hôtel later that day. [17]

Claude Perreault, Footman (Michener)

---

17   Claude Perreault, Footman, Employee Reunion collection, 1992

SALADS AND SMILES

I recall one occasion during a state dinner where the salad course on the menu read as follows: "Salade au hasard du marché et aux pignons." The key word to understand in this phrase is "pignons," which, when translated into English, means pine nuts, a variety of tiny gourmet nuts, harvested from pine trees, often used in specialty dishes.

An elderly gentleman, intrigued by the meaning of the word "pignons" politely drew the attention of one of the footmen in the Ballroom and asked the meaning of the word. The footman, more than happy to respond to the gentleman's question, replied "Sir, those are pigeon nuts." Naturally, everyone at the table looked at each other with intrigue. After some clarification, everyone was able to enjoy the salad, to my relief![18]

Executive Chef Stephen D. Gervais (Hnatyshyn mandate)

---

18   Stephen D. Gervais, Executive Chef, from Employee Reunion Collection, 1992

OFFICE LUNCH ETIQUETTE

My first year at Rideau Hall included the last six months of the Léger mandate and the arrival of the Schreyers. Early into the new mandate, Mr. Schreyer decided that he would hold informal luncheons in the greenhouse with four or five staff members at a time, to learn more about their role and the work they did. One morning, I was informed by the aide-de-camp that my brown bag lunch that day would have to wait, since I, along with a few other people, was going to lunch with His Excellency. Naturally, lunching with the Governor General is not something one does every day, especially given that, less than a year earlier, I was a student living on fast food and pizza! My immediate concern, however, was getting a quick course on 'Dining with Dignitaries 101.' Since nobody had even heard about 'Google' back then, I scrambled around asking about which of the many forks to use just in case we were served prawns!

When came the time for lunch, the aide-de-camp arrived at my office to accompany me to the greenhouse, where we were all seated at a beautifully dressed round table. I can still remember the scent of the spring flowers while watching the falling snowflakes through the glass panes of the greenhouse. It felt like we were in a snow globe.

Introductions were made and, soon after, the footmen arrived with large silver platters covered with shiny domes. When the maître d'hôtel gave the signal, the domes were removed to reveal hamburgers, hot dogs and French fries! Not only was I surprised but also relieved that we would not be having something that I couldn't pronounce, let alone digest! And I was even more relieved when the Governor General reached for his burger and took a bite! I breathed a sigh of relief and enjoyed the rest of the meal.

Gabrielle Lappa

STYLES OF ADDRESS

When I first started at Rideau Hall in 1982, I was the secretary to Mr. Esmond Butler who was the Secretary to the Governor General. I was also the Francophone secretary to Governor General Edward Schreyer.

On my first day at Rideau Hall, Elizabeth Pitney, Mr. Schreyer's Anglophone secretary, coached me on how to address the Governor General which is "Your Excellency." I kept repeating this to myself until I came face to face with Mr. Schreyer and greeted him as "Your Highness." I noticed that he ignored it but tried to stifle a laugh. We continued our conversation as we walked towards his office when, for a second time, I promoted him to "Your Majesty." Again, being very polite, Mr. Schreyer ignored it and tried not to laugh. In his office, the Governor General sat in a chair by the fireplace and invited me to sit on the love seat across from him. As I went to sit on the small sofa, I sank into the down-filled cushions which felt to me like I was almost sitting on the floor. I landed with both legs up in the air and let out a startled cry of "My God," to which Mr. Schreyer calmly replied "That's OK. Just call me Mr. Schreyer."

Louise Cléroux, 23 years of service

A MOMENT IN HISTORY

The state funeral for the 15th Canadian Prime Minister, the Right Honourable Pierre Trudeau, was held on October 3, 2000, at the Notre-Dame Basilica in Montréal. As for all state funerals, the Department of Canadian Heritage, formerly Secretary of State, was responsible for coordinating the necessary arrangements. Following the funeral service, a reception was to take place at a nearby venue, hosted by Governor General Adrienne Clarkson. Because of the size of the event and the many dignitaries expected, a few of our staff members were asked to assist with the guests at the reception. We were each assigned a responsibility and told where and when to be in place. I was to be in the VIP reception room where the world leaders and high-level dignitaries attending the funeral would meet for a small gathering with the family. My job was to greet the guests and ensure that only those on my list had access to the room.

As the funeral ended, we all took our places. It took some time for the guests to arrive, so I waited alone in the reception room, enjoying the view of Old Montréal. Hearing someone entering the room, I turned and came face to face with the first guest – Fidel Castro, the President of Cuba. He was a tall, handsome man, dressed in a suit instead of the legendary khakis which he was usually photographed wearing and, for a brief moment, which seemed longer, all I could think was that my usual "Hello and thank you for coming" was just not appropriate. Whatever controversy may have surrounded the man and his policies, he was there on this day to pay tribute to a friend and to see the family. I invited Mr. Castro to have a refreshment while waiting for the others to arrive and, not surprisingly, he was most gracious, taking a glass of sparkling water and moving to the window to admire the magnificent view. Within moments, the other dignitaries began to arrive, and I quietly stepped back and watched this gathering of world leaders who had come to pay their respects to a great Canadian. It was a surreal moment and one that I will never forget.

Gabrielle Lappa

PAR 3 GOLF

Towards the end of one of our famous aides-de-camp parties, I grabbed a couple of putters and a practice putting hole and convinced one of our guests to play Rideau Hall mini-golf with me. Making up the holes as we went, they ranged from par 2 to par 6, from the third floor where we had our living quarters, down to the first floor, from one end of the Ballroom to the other end of the Long Gallery and from the ADCs offices to the Greenhouses, via the staff offices. On one of the shots that my opponent took down the long office corridor leading to the Greenhouse, the ball ricocheted off the railing and exited the Greenhouse through one of the windowpanes. In a nervous voice, he asked what he should do. I calmly replied, "Take a drop and a one-stroke penalty!"

Fortunately, when we returned to our apartment, Ed Lawrence, our head gardener, was still there and the minor mishap was remedied the next morning![19]

Captain Mark Phillips, Aide-de-Camp to Madame Sauvé

---

19   Capt. Mark Phillips, Aide-de-Camp, from the Employee Reunion Collection, 1992

HOCKEY NIGHT ON THE TRAINS!

For seven years, we crossed Canada several times. It was memorable how General Vanier would bear up during such long hours wearing his uniform, especially in the summer. When he would return to the train, he was literally soaked with perspiration, but he always had a kind word and a smile for the porter and for me as he boarded the train.

While travelling during the winter months, if His Excellency did not have an evening engagement, we would all be invited to join him in the sitting room of car #1 to watch the hockey game and his favorite team, Les Canadiens de Montréal.[20]

Wilfred Notley, C.M., Chief Steward

---

20   Wilfred Notley, Chief Steward, Excerpt from Employee Reunion Collection, 1992

CHILDHOOD MEMORIES

One of my first childhood memories is at Rideau Hall. During the sixties, my father, Ben Tracey, was the Greenhouse Supervisor and our family of eight lived on the grounds. At Christmas, Madame Vanier always enjoyed visiting the families who lived there. I remember how nervous my parents always were, worried primarily about the behaviour of their six children. However, any concern that might have existed before the visit dissipated within moments of Madame Vanier's entrance as she quickly gathered up one of my brothers on her knee and spent time chatting with us all. I also recall Mrs. Michener coming to visit our home during the winter. As she was getting ready to leave, my father offered Her Excellency a chair to use as she was putting on her boots. Mrs. Michener quickly rejected the offer, saying that a true Canadian can put on winter boots while standing!

The annual Christmas gatherings for the employees and their families were always special. On a few occasions, I recall that we were entertained by a child pianist who has since become a world-renowned performer named Angela Hewitt.

Many years later, I started to work at Rideau Hall in what was called the Central Registry and Anniversaries Section. My job was to send out anniversary and birthday telegrams from the Governor General to those reaching milestone years. It was a rewarding and important job especially for those Canadians who received the messages.

During his mandate, I recall Mr. Michener often making impromptu visits to the office staff. We would sometimes receive a two-minute warning from an aide-de-camp that His Excellency was on his way. Our office was located on the third floor of the Administration Wing and Mr. Michener would climb those stairs two-at-a-time to reach our perch. He knew all our names and would spend about ten minutes with us before he was off again like the wind! For a number of years, after the end of his mandate, Mr. Michener would come to Rideau Hall and often visit the employees in their offices, always with a box of chocolates in hand for us to enjoy.

Pat (Tracey) McRae, Research Officer, Information Management, 37 years of service

THE LITTLE LOST BEAR

The Annual Teddy Bear Picnic for the Children's Hospital of Eastern Ontario (CHEO) is a long-standing tradition held every summer in Ottawa. The event used to take place at a public park in the city, and thousands of visitors would enjoy a fun-filled day of activities organized by the CHEO Foundation and by the many volunteers and employees of the hospital.

During the LeBlanc mandate, the suggestion was made to organizers to move the annual event to Rideau Hall where children could enjoy the park-like setting and yet be "contained" within the perimeters of the grounds! Mr. LeBlanc enjoyed seeing young families on the property. Soon after his installation as Governor General, he asked that a large wooden play structure be added to the grounds, next to the Visitors' Centre, for children to enjoy.

The first year of the Teddy Bear Picnic at Rideau Hall was a great success, with numbers surpassing previous years. A petting zoo, mini train rides throughout the grounds, food and refreshment areas, face painting and clowns kept everyone busy. But the most popular spot, by far, was the BASH tent (Bear Army Surgical Hospital) where injured teddy bears, dolls and stuffed animals could be seen by doctors and nurses for a proper diagnosis. The line-up for the patients and their guardians was always the longest.

That year, a prominent visitor attended the event with his young granddaughter who was concerned about her injured bear. After a busy afternoon, the event was coming to an end and the "surgeons" could not see any more patients. A friend of the visitor in question, who also happened to be the president of the CHEO Foundation, assured the little girl that he would personally take care of her bear and have it returned to her as soon as its injuries were repaired. Unfortunately, more than a few days passed, and the bear was set aside during a brief summer vacation. A few weeks later, I received a call from Mrs. LeBlanc, asking if I knew the status of the bear that was left behind at the CHEO picnic, and when could the little girl expect to get it back. This was clearly one of those moments best described as "other related duties!" Undeterred by the unusual request, I offered to contact the bear's family to let them know that we were looking into the matter and were prepared to seek help from the RCMP if necessary! A quick phone call to the CHEO Foundation offices reassured me that the bear was not lost, just placed in "intensive care" while a few people went on vacation! The saga became even funnier as we realized that a teddy bear had actually ended up in a real hospital to be mended! Within a few days, the bear was released from hospital, fully recovered and returned to one very happy little girl!

Gabrielle Lappa, Policy and Planning Team

COCKTAILS AND CAMPERS

Following Mr. Léger's stroke, just months after his installation as Governor General, Madame Léger never left his side, stepping in to deliver his messages when he could not. His period of rehabilitation was quite lengthy, and we, the staff, did all we could to support the Légers who considered us their family. One of the aides who lived in Rideau Hall had purchased a large camper, the driving kind. He loved to boast about his camper which was also his home away from Rideau Hall. Anxious to show his prized possession to the Légers, all of us devised a plan to help him out.

The inside of the camper was turned into a formal "cocktail lounge" and all we needed to do was to find a way to get Their Excellencies into the camper where they would have their pre-dinner cocktails that evening. The aide pulled the camper up onto the sidewalk, as close as possible to the side entrance so there was very little space between the Residence door and the step leading into the camper. When the aide-de-camp called on Their Excellencies to come down for cocktails, he announced that the route would be slightly different than the one they took each night since the drinks would be served in another room. Mr. Léger wondered aloud where we were taking him until he stepped into the camper and everyone burst into laughter! That evening, we all joined Their Excellencies for cocktails in the camper before returning inside for dinner. It was likely one of the most memorable evenings for the Légers, with their adopted family!

Richard Legrand, Footman

LIVE FROM RIDEAU HALL / EN DIRECT DE RIDEAU HALL

The year 2002 marked the 50ᵗʰ anniversary of the appointment of the first Canadian Governor General, the Rt. Hon. Vincent Massey, in 1952. Governor General Adrienne Clarkson loved to celebrate Canada and its artists and felt that something should be done to mark this important anniversary in the history of the Office and of Rideau Hall.

The Governor General's Summer Concert Series had been launched 10 years earlier during the Hnatyshyn mandate and much work had been done to make the Office and the Residence more visible, more inviting, and more accessible to the public. The idea of a star-studded all-Canadian concert became a reality when an independent producer, Lynn Harvey, confirmed that the CBC would assist with the cost and production of the event and that it would be televised live from Rideau Hall. Adrienne Clarkson was delighted and called in her favours with some of Canada's top performers by phoning and sending personal letters to all of them.

"Live from Rideau Hall / En direct de Rideau Hall" was one of the most rewarding and yet most challenging projects of my career. For the first six months of 2002, a small team worked almost full time on the arrangements. The Governor General personally phoned and wrote to artists like Gordon Lightfoot, Stompin' Tom Connors, Measha Brueggergosman, Mario Pelchat and The Barenaked Ladies, who all agreed to perform at the outdoor concert. Even the National Arts Centre Orchestra, conducted by Mario Bernardi, agreed to be a key part of the all-Canadian line-up.

A week before the event, we watched as the three concert stages, all connected with a colorful royal blue background, began to go up. Inside the Residence, the events and implementation teams were converting the elegant Ballroom and Tent Room into small individual dressing rooms, separated by curtains and fully stocked with the necessary amenities. It looked like they did this once a week and yet it was a first for Rideau Hall. Four days before the event, all the arrangements were progressing as planned. The executive producer, Lynn Harvey, and the CBC team were a pleasure to work with. And the Rideau Hall team worked as if producing television shows was their real job!

And then it started to rain. All day. And the next day. And the next. The day before the event, a few hours before the dress rehearsal was scheduled to begin, a large production truck got stuck in the mud which now covered the pristine grounds of Rideau Hall. My long-time colleague, Duncan Mousseau, tried to control the logistical nightmare as equipment everywhere was being covered with plastic tarps. Even the crew joked about having to build an ark! And as if the rain was not enough, the traditionally warmer weather in mid-June was replaced by cool winds. At this point, I had stopped wearing a suit and high heels and my official wardrobe became yellow mud-covered rainboots, a ghastly purple hooded raincoat, and layers of sweaters and jeans to keep me warm. Far from our usual dress code!

By mid-afternoon, a few hours before the performers were scheduled to arrive for the dress rehearsal, I was in the Governor General's office, providing her with the latest update on weather reports and catastrophic occurrences at the concert site, when there was a knock on the door. In came Gordon Lightfoot, the singer/songwriter whose music, including my favorite, "A Song for a Winter's Night," had taken me and my roommates through our university years of late-night essay writing and cramming for exams. In 1976, we had pooled our savings to buy tickets for Lightfoot's show at the National Arts Centre. We were true fans. And there I was, wearing my yellow rain boots and purple raincoat, with wet hair and runny mascara. I was ready to hide under the Governor General's desk!

Adrienne Clarkson was so happy to see her long-time friend and introduced me to Mr. Lightfoot! His genuine charm and friendly smile warmed the chill in my bones and, hearing him perform "If you could read my mind" at the dress rehearsal was exactly what we all needed to warm our hearts.

The rain continued throughout the night as well as on the morning of the show. The CBC had invested so much time and money in this production that, as long as there wasn't lightening in the sky, the show was going to go ahead. And then, just hours before the show was scheduled to begin, the sun appeared. The groundskeepers from the National Capital Commission decided to lay dry straw on the muddy grass where chairs for the VIPs were being set up. Crowds of people started streaming through the gates with chairs and blankets and picnics. Everything and everyone came together like clockwork and, to quote the Governor General that day, "The show must go on!"

The concert was a blend of great performers who presented a beautiful mix of all genres of music, from opera to country to pop, in both languages, and Adrienne Clarkson was the perfect host. Unfortunately, for the VIPs seated close to the stage where the NCC had laid down the dry straw to absorb the moisture from the rain, the fleas embedded in the straw came alive partway through the show and anyone with bare legs or arms spent the better part of the concert scratching or swatting away the little beasties! Fortunately, that part was not caught on camera!

RIDEAU HALL
OTTAWA

THE GOVERNOR GENERAL
LA GOUVERNEURE GÉNÉRALE

July 2, 2002

Dear Tom,

What a good friend you are! Your performance at the Rideau Hall concert was more than generous, and I can't tell you how much I appreciate your kindness.

It all turned out so well. The rain and the mud were such a plague and, at times, I worried that the whole concert would be washed out. But then, in typical Canadian fashion, we made a compromise with the weather and the show went on. And it was a brilliant success!

That night you were, as you always will be, the perfect opening for an evening of Canadian music. And I am forever your fan and grateful friend.

Affectionately yours,

Adrienne Clarkson

Stompin' Tom Connors, O.C.

Governor General Adrienne Clarkson with Gordon Lightfoot, Susan Aglukark, Natalie MacMaster and other top Canadian performers at the "Live from Rideau Hall" concert in 2002. Photo credit: Rideau Hall photographer

Following the concert, all the performers gathered inside the Residence to unwind, enjoy the hospitality and jam with their fellow performers. The party went on well into the night and, as tired as we all were, we were happy to be able to share a little bit of Rideau Hall's history with the rest of the country.

The next day, I received a message from the Creative Head of the CBC, George Anthony, which started with "We won the night!", meaning that no other show on air that night was watched by as many people! In George's own words "A piece of cake, it wasn't. Well worth doing, it was."

Gabrielle Lappa, Director, Policy and Planning

LONG DRIVE, SHORT PUTT

I became the first female officer of the Household on August 15, 1979. Two weeks later, I was told I would have to go to the Citadelle because Their Excellencies would need Francophone staff in Québec. I still needed a map to find my office in the labyrinth that is Rideau Hall and was not overly enthusiastic at the prospect of being uprooted so soon. However, orders are orders! I must say that, as soon as I saw the Citadelle, I fell hopelessly, utterly and irretrievably in love with the place although the house still bore the scars of the dreadful 1976 fire.

Mr. Schreyer was scheduled to give a speech in Victoriaville and, as the speech was to be given entirely in French, I knew I would have to write it. However, I simply could not get in to see His Excellency to ask him the topics he wished to discuss on that occasion, and I was still too new on staff to feel comfortable about starting on a draft without consultation. Time was getting short, and I was becoming downright desperate.

I mentioned my problem to one of the ADCs, then Captain Bernard St-Laurent, who was entirely at home at the Citadelle as he was a proud member of the Vandoos (the Royal 22ᵉ Régiment). Captain St-Laurent was blessed with immense resourcefulness coupled with a mischievous sense of humor. He told me to be at the front door the following morning at 9:30 sharp. His Excellency was scheduled to play golf that day.

I showed up the next morning and was told by Captain St-Laurent to get into the back seat of the waiting limousine. Shortly thereafter,

His Excellency arrived and, seeing me sitting in the car; an expression of quiet resignation came over his face. He shot Captain St-Laurent a dirty look but made no comment as he got into the limo. We drove off and I started asking His Excellency about possible topics for the speech. Graciously accepting defeat, he started to talk while I scribbled furiously, afraid to miss a word. We drove and drove, and His Excellency talked. Eventually, I had enough material to be able to prepare something useful. Once our conversation had turned to weather and other mundane matters, the ADC gave the driver the signal to enter the golf course. The chauffeur handed the clubs to the aide-de-camp and off they went! On the way back to the Citadelle, I remarked to the chauffeur how short the drive back had been. Jean Chouinard, the driver, burst out laughing as he told me that he had been told by the ADC to keep driving as long as His Excellency was talking. He had been circling the course for half an hour! I'm not sure if Mr. Schreyer ever noticed that he had been kidnapped by his own staff but, in the end, it worked!

Jeanne G. Marsolais, Speechwriter during the Schreyer and Sauvé mandates.

AN UNKEPT BED

It was 1967, Canada's Centennial Year, when more than 60 royals and heads of state from around the world came to pay homage to Canada and to admire its beauty and its achievements. Of all the state visits during Centennial Year, it seemed that none was planned more meticulously than that of General de Gaulle. Starting with Monsieur Zonda, the French Chef who had been at Government House since the days of Governor General Massey, everyone was feverishly preparing themselves for the great visit. Monsieur Zonda had reached retirement age, yet he had agreed to stay on until the end of the year when the state visits would be over. He was an exceptional chef who made Canada proud at every state dinner he produced.

I recall the ambassador of France paying a call on Their Excellencies to discuss arrangements several weeks before the General's visit. He was shown the Royal Suite where the General and Madame de Gaulle would spend the night. The Suite had been completely redecorated and the bathrooms refurbished, fixtures and all. The ambassador pointed out that the bed in the Royal Suite was too short to accommodate the General who measured close to 6'10". The carpenters at Government House went to work and soon a wooden extension was produced according to the Ambassador's specifications.

Their Excellencies went to Québec to receive the General and Madame de Gaulle. Those of us who accompanied them joined them at the Citadelle to watch the French cruiser, *Colbert*, with the General on board, silently approaching the city. The General and Madame de Gaulle were officially welcomed to Canada by the Queen's representative and offered refreshments at the Citadelle, before proceeding by road to Montréal.

As history records, "Vive le Québec! Vive le Québec libre!" was uttered by the General from the balcony of Montréal's City Hall, while Their Excellencies sped to Ottawa to receive him in the nation's capital. We know that the General never made it to Ottawa. Several months later, while going through the gift room in the basement of Government House, I saw, propped up against the wall, a large wooden extension for a bed with "de Gaulle" written on it in large letters. I stopped and looked at it for a moment. I had before me a reminder of a turning point in Canadian history. [21]

Helen Webster, LVO (Lady-in-Waiting for Mrs. Norah Michener)

---

21   Helen Webster, LVO, Lady-in-Waiting, from Employee Reunion Collection, 1992

BURGERS WITH THE BOYS!

It was Madame Sauvé's birthday, with no official activities planned as her husband was out of town. So, we (the aides-de-camp) decided to take matters into our own hands to celebrate Her Excellency's birthday. With a quick, last minute call to the RCMP to advise them of an unexpected outing, we invited Madame Sauvé to come down to see us. When she did, we told her she was going for a ride – in Luc Maurice's K-car, a scary prospect on its own! We quickly pulled out of Rideau Hall, just as the RCMP bodyguards were pulling in.

Driving along Sussex Drive with the RCMP trying to catch up, we realized the security breach that we would likely pay for, but Madame Sauvé was enjoying the adventure and nothing else mattered. We soon realized that we had missed the turn-off for the MacDonald-Cartier bridge which would take us towards Hull in Quebec. After a bit of a detour, we finally reached our destination, a small restaurant up in the Gatineau Hills, with just a minor dent when Luc tried to park his K-car. Her Excellency laughed so much as she was treated to a gourmet birthday burger and a fun evening with her boys![22]

Capt. Marc Philips, Aide-de-Camp to the Rt. Hon. Jeanne Sauvé

---

22   Capt. Marc Philips, Aide-de-Camp, from the Employee Reunion Collection, 1992

THE MOVING CLOCK

During the Queen's Jubilee Tour of Canada in 1977, the Queen and Prince Philip stayed at Rideau Hall with the Légers. Her Majesty had indicated that she would like to meet then-Prime Minister Pierre Trudeau's children. When Mr. Trudeau and the children arrived, the Queen had requested a rather informal gathering, so they all sat in the small drawing room along the main corridor. Towards the end of their chat, the group wandered into the hallway which led to the gardens. Against the wall was a rather large grandfather clock. Her Majesty was engaged in conversation with Mr. Trudeau, with her back to the clock, when the clock started to move.

One of the youngest Trudeau children had been scampering around on the carpet at the base of the clock and had somehow managed to dislodge it. My look of horror must have signaled to the Queen that something was terribly wrong, as she turned and straight-armed the clock when it was within inches of hitting her on the head! To her credit, Her Majesty did not miss a beat and left me with the task of securing the clock in its rightful position while she wandered off with Mr. Trudeau and the children. [23]

David C. Summers, Aide-de-Camp (Michener, Léger)

---

23   David C. Summers, Aide-de-Camp, from the Employee Reunion Collection, 1992

CLOSING A CHAPTER

We were nearing the end of the Governor General's mandate and, as is always the case, these days are filled with farewell events, receptions, and dinners. I was scheduled to be away on Their Excellencies' last day so, during a quiet moment the day before, I thanked them and told them that it had been a real pleasure for me to work with them and their family during the past five years. The Governor General looked at me strangely and said "Why Tim? Where are you going?" Without thinking, I replied "I'm not going anywhere but you are." Fortunately, they had a sense of humour and laughed at my unexpected reply. Before long, they would, once again, be adjusting to life outside of Rideau Hall and we would be welcoming the new residents to "One Sussex Drive."

Tim Roberge, Footman

Gerda Hnatyshyn with staff members. Left to right: Gabrielle Lappa, Annick Brie, Paulette Bélisle, Thérèse Rochefort, Richard Berthelsen and Nancy Davies (seated) Photo credit: Bertrand Thibeault.

BIBLIOGRAPHY

Arcand, Ted J., *Protocol Manual, Government House*, Ottawa, 1994

Bryant, Joyce, C.M., BEM, *Slender Threads, A Memoir,* Ottawa, 2007

Clarkson, Adrienne and John Ralston Saul, with Margaret MacMillan, Marjorie Harris, Anne L.Desjardins, *Rideau Hall And The Invention of a Canadian Home,* Alfred A. Knopf Canada, Toronto, 2004

Clarkson, Adrienne, *Heart Matters,* Penguin Random House Canada, Toronto, 2006

Coady, Mary Frances, *Georges and Pauline Vanier, Portrait of a Couple*, McGill-Queen's University Press, Montréal, 2011

Earle, Tom, *An interview with Esmond Butler*, Library of Parliament, Ottawa, September 1988

Hnatyshyn, Gerda, *Rideau Hall, Canada's Living Heritage*, Friesen Press, Ottawa, 1994

Lascelles, A.F., *Government House*, Ottawa, 1934

McCreery, Christopher, *Fifty Years Honouring Canadians: The Order of Canada, 1967-2017,* Dundurn, Toronto, 2017

THE AUTHOR

G abrielle Lappa has always enjoyed reading and writing stories about lives lived. She was born in Cornwall, Ontario, to parents who emigrated from Italy and made Canada their home. After completing her studies at Carleton University, she accepted a short-term position at Rideau Hall and stayed for thirty-six years. During that time, she worked for eight governors general, first with the Program Planning team, later as the Director of Policy and Planning and, for the last seven years, as the Director of Honours. She was awarded the Queen's Silver and Golden Jubilee medals as well as the Vice-Regal Commendation for service to the Office. She retired from Rideau Hall in 2014 and enjoys writing about the interesting people in her world. Gabrielle makes her home in Manotick, Ontario. (lappagabrielle@gmail.com)

CPSIA information can be obtained
at www.ICGtesting.com
Printed in the USA
BVHW050807191021
619299BV00014B/522/J